# A Cross-Stitch
# CHRISTMAS®

## Warmest Wishes

Craftways® Corporation
Stevens Point, WI

# A Cross-Stitch CHRISTMAS

**Maureen Ruth**
Publishing Director

**Jennifer Mitchell**
Editor-in-Chief

**Jennifer Milner**
Publications Editor

**Stephanie Tahtinen**
Assistant Editor

**Amber Olszewski**
Art Director

**Communication Logistics, Inc.**
Creative Services

**Pinky Betts, Megan Clawson, Amanda Fichter, Twila Fickel, Rebekah Hook, Bonnie Hope, Becky Lemoine, Ayn Locklear, Rene Massey, Jan Meachen, Amy Meyer, Peggy O'Hara, Judy Osterhoudt, Robyn Purta, Pamela Ray, Lois Schultz, Shanna Senecal, Carol Stonecipher, Mellody Valencia, Chanda VanDuser, Karyl Vislay, Betsy Warner**
Stitchers and Finishers

**Sarah Schmidt**
Director of Business Development

**Kati Heil**
Marketing Manager

**Jacob Polak**
Business Analyst

**Jena Carlin Creative**
Photography

For book editorial questions, write
Craftways Corporation A Cross-Stitch Christmas® 2020
PO Box 761, Stevens Point, WI 54481
**For additional copies or billing questions,** call 1-800-713-1239

# *There is truly something special about the holiday season.*

You can feel it in the air: everyone is a little readier to laugh, celebrate, forgive, and be thankful. When the snow starts to fall and the weather gets colder, when holiday music can be heard in stores and restaurants, when kids and adults alike start thinking about a little respite from the daily routine, we know that Christmas is on its way.

Suddenly we are looking forward to connecting with family and friends, eating our favorite foods, and watching our favorite movies. We share old traditions and make new memories that become part of our holiday experience. We bring out the stockings and mistletoe and exchange gifts in the light of the Christmas tree. Our hearts and minds are filled in the pleasant way unique to this time of year. Within these pages are projects created by individuals who love Christmas just as much as you do. We joyfully select pieces in a wide variety of styles, colors, and skill levels so you can get that holiday feeling no matter if you are just starting out with a bright aesthetic or have been stitching for years and prefer something traditional. With so many options to choose from, we know you are going to create pieces of art filled with

# Warmest Wishes.

# *A Cross-Stitch Christmas®*
# Contents

Let this masterful collection of classic and contemporary cross-stitch themes delight your senses as you stitch and create in the Spirit of Christmas.

66

91

29

9

46

112

# Celebrating Santa

*Father Christmas, Kris Kringle, the Jolly Old Elf; however you know him, Santa Claus is a treasured and beloved character in our holiday stories.* He doesn't always look the same, but you can always find him spreading love, charity, and joy at the Christmas season. Fly away with this musical Santa created by Malaysian designer Vinniey Tan, or depict him on a snowy stocking, with vibrant vintage style, or in a traditional portrait with beautiful, realistic detail. Whatever you stitch, you'll be creating a piece of needlework worthy of the nice list!

**Project instructions begin on page 17.**

*Explore Santa's childlike wonder with this set of three funky bookmarks* designed by Barbara Campagna. His silly antics will have you smiling all season long.

**Project instructions begin on page 16.**

# Celebrating Santa

*Enjoy some time in the snowy forest with this jolly little Santa Claus* designed by Becky Spencer. His kind smile will welcome friends and family from his place of honor on the mantel.

**Project instructions begin on page 13.**

*Old-world style radiates from these adorable pie tin cushion ornaments* designed by Cecilia Turner. From bald in blue to lighting the way in a long cap, these designs show off all of Santa's looks.

**Project instructions begin on page 22.**

*You'll be amazed by the stunning adaptation of artwork* by Tom Wood into a brilliant cross-stitch portrait by Barbara Ana. With beautiful shading and amazing attention to detail, this portrait is a show-stopper.

**Project instructions begin on page 20.**

# Celebrating Santa

*Santa and the Mrs. are out for date night at a snow globe skating rink* in this cute pattern designed by Lee Fisher. A shadow box and some pom-poms give this unique design a snowy setting of its own.

**Project instructions begin on page 23.**

# Celebrating Santa

## Forest Santa Stocking

### Fabric
- One 18" × 21" piece of 14-ct. White Aida

### Design Size
- 14-ct. = 9⅜" × 14¼"

### Finishing Materials
- 1 yard of blue print fabric for lining and back
- 1½ yards of ¼"-wide cording
- Matching sewing thread

### General Instructions
Center the design and begin stitching. Work cross-stitches with two strands of cotton embroidery floss or DMC® Light Effects floss. Work backstitches with one strand of cotton embroidery floss or DMC Light Effects floss. Use a pressing cloth to carefully iron the needlework from the back before finishing.

### Finishing Instructions
Use a ½" seam allowance for all sewing unless otherwise specified. Center and trim the needlework to within 1½" of the stitching on the top edge and to within ½" of the stitching around the sides and bottom. With the wrong side up, use the needlework as a template to cut two pieces from the right side of blue fabric. Flip the needlework right side up and use it as a template to cut one piece from the right side of blue fabric.

Cut 1½"-wide bias strips of blue fabric and piece together to form one 40"-long strip. Fold in half lengthwise with wrong sides together. Insert cording into the fold and sew tightly along the edge of the cording using a zipper foot. Making sure the cording is flush with the edge of the stitching, start at the top left of the needlework and sew the piping around the stocking, keeping the seam close to the cording.

With right sides together, sew the stocking front to the back, sewing tight to the cording but leaving the top open. Trim the side and bottom seam allowances to ¼". Turn the stocking right side out and press.

Sew the lining pieces together in the same manner as the stocking, but use a 1" seam allowance and leave a 4" opening along the bottom of the "foot" for turning. Trim the side and bottom seam allowances to ¼".

Leave the lining wrong side out and insert the stocking into the lining, aligning the top edges. Sew all the way around the top, sewing through all layers. Pull the stocking through the opening in the lining and slipstitch the opening closed. Tuck the lining inside the stocking and press.

Cut a 2½" × 9" strip of blue fabric for the hanging loop. Turn each long edge ¼" to the wrong side and press. Fold in half lengthwise and press. Topstitch ⅛" away from the long edge. Attach to the top right inner corner of the stocking with a few hand-stitches.

# Celebrating
# Santa

## Project Tip

### Sewing Not Your Thing?
Talk to your local needlework store about recommending a finishing service. A good finisher can either complete the stocking as we've shown here or suggest one of the many other ways your piece could be finished. Some options might include a lace cuff or a cording trim. Or, if you would like to learn how to finish your own needlework, contact a local fabric or quilt store to inquire about sewing classes. You just might find a new passion!

### CROSS-STITCH

| ANCHOR | | DMC | COLOR |
|---|---|---|---|
| 387 | C | Ecru | Ecru |
| 400 | T | 317 | Pewter Gray |
| 011 | A | 350 | Medium Coral |
| 1045 | B | 436 | Tan |
| 362 | W | 437 | Light Tan |
| 293 | J | 727 | Very Light Topaz |
| 387 | Z | 739 | Ultra Very Light Tan |
| 128 | N | 775 | Very Light Baby Blue |
| 132 | R | 797 | Royal Blue |
| 131 | I | 798 | Dark Delft Blue |
| 136 | L | 799 | Medium Delft Blue |
| 013 | H | 817 | Very Dark Coral Red |
| 229 | G | 910 | Dark Emerald Green |
| 205 | K | 911 | Medium Emerald Green |
| 204 | V | 913 | Medium Nile Green |
| 1011 | S | 948 | Very Light Peach |
| 203 | E | 954 | Nile Green |
| 129 | F | 3325 | Light Baby Blue |
| 1020 | U | 3713 | Very Light Salmon |
| 1037 | Y | 3756 | Ultra Very Light Baby Blue |
| 1009 | P | 3770 | Very Light Tawny |
| 236 | X | 3799 | Very Dark Pewter Gray |
| 002 | O | 3865 | Winter White |

| DMC LIGHT EFFECTS | | COLOR |
|---|---|---|
| 3852 | D | Gold Metallic |

### BACKSTITCH

| ANCHOR | | DMC | COLOR |
|---|---|---|---|
| 236 | —— | 3799 | Very Dark Pewter Gray |

| DMC LIGHT EFFECTS | COLOR |
|---|---|
| 3852 —— | Gold Metallic |

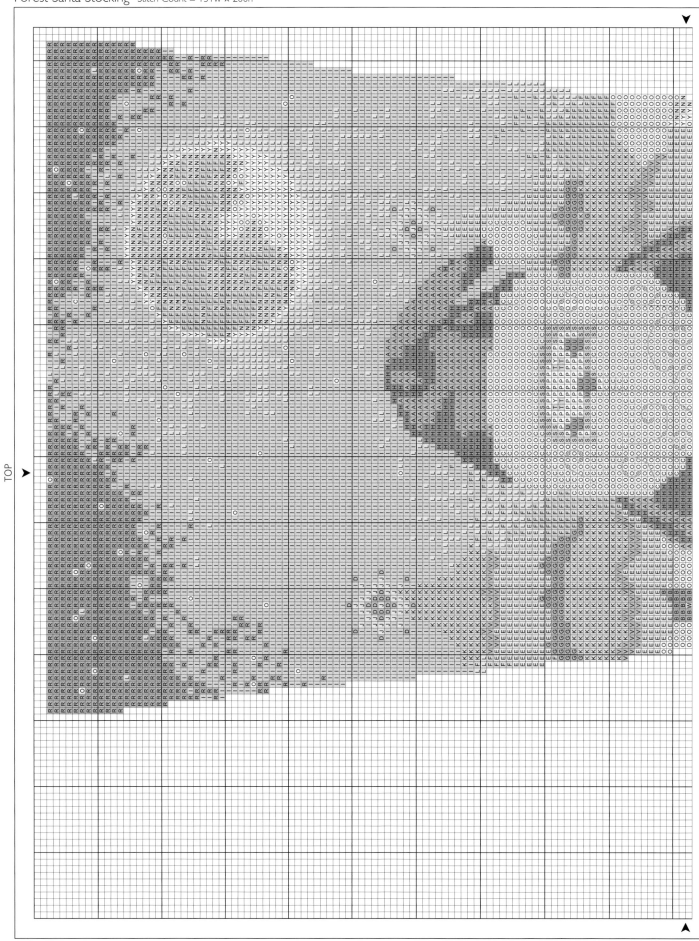

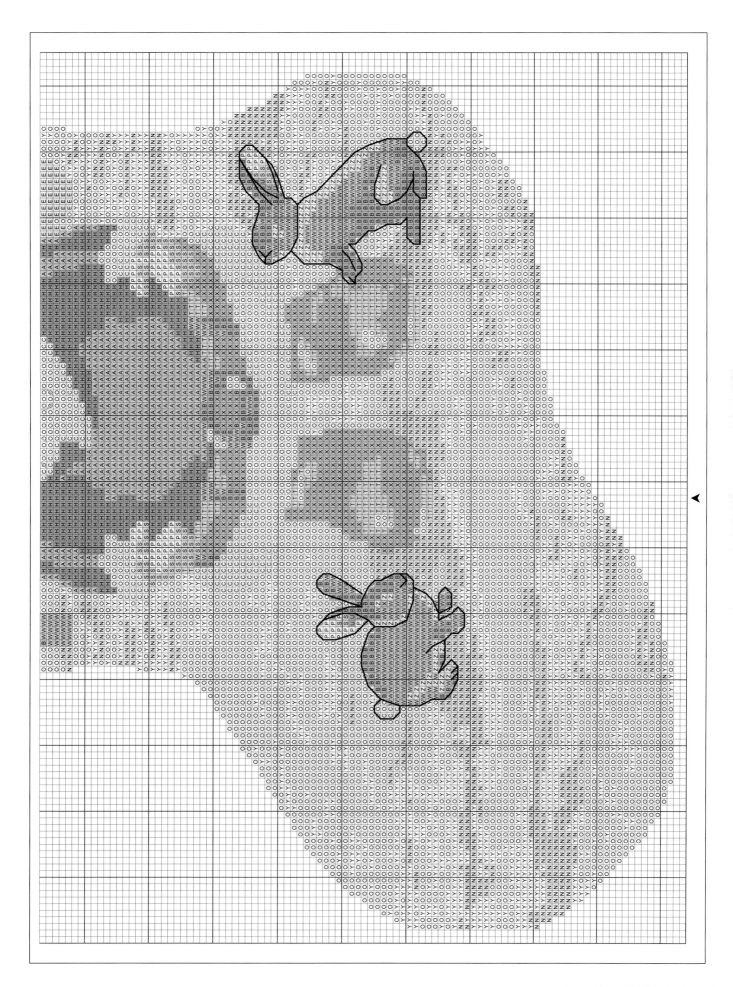

## Bookmark 1 · Stitch Count = 28w × 70h

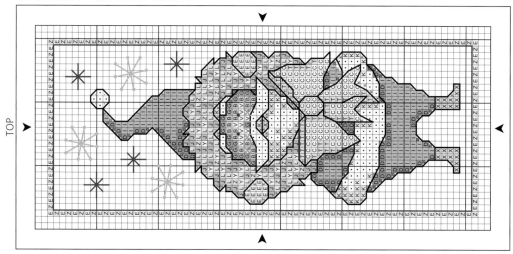

## Bookmark 2 · Stitch Count = 28w × 70h

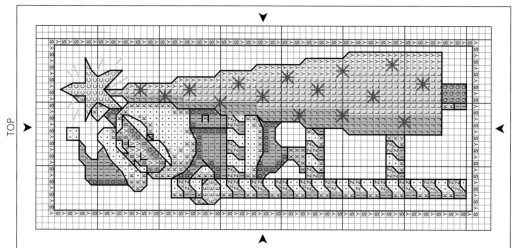

## Bookmark 3 · Stitch Count = 28w × 70h

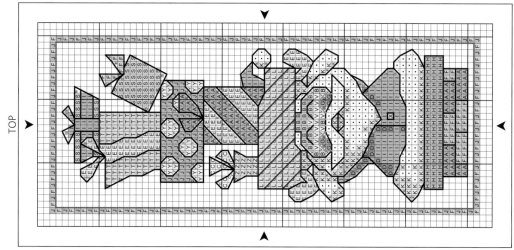

### CROSS-STITCH

| ANCHOR | | DMC | COLOR |
|---|---|---|---|
| 002 | · | White | White |
| 280 | Y | 166 | Medium Light Moss Gree |
| 403 | X | 310 | Black |
| 9046 | I | 321 | Christmas Red |
| 358 | Q | 433 | Medium Brown |
| 281 | J | 580 | Dark Moss Green |
| 280 | L | 581 | Moss Green |
| 273 | H | 645 | Very Dark Beaver Gray |
| 046 | Z | 666 | Bright Christmas Red |
| 326 | A | 720 | Dark Orange Spice |
| 324 | F | 721 | Medium Orange Spice |
| 305 | C | 728 | Topaz |
| 303 | T | 742 | Light Tangerine |
| 1012 | B | 754 | Light Peach |
| 234 | K | 762 | Very Light Pearl Gray |
| 043 | D | 815 | Medium Garnet |
| 1011 | V | 948 | Very Light Peach |
| 1013 | G | 3778 | Light Terra Cotta |
| 1076 | S | 3847 | Dark Teal Green |
| 1070 | E | 3849 | Light Teal Green |

### FRENCH KNOT

| ANCHOR | | DMC | COLOR |
|---|---|---|---|
| 403 | ● | 310 | Black |
| 1076 | ● | 3847 | Dark Teal Green |

### BACKSTITCH

| ANCHOR | | DMC | COLOR |
|---|---|---|---|
| 403 | —— | 310 | Black |
| 281 | —— | 580 | Dark Moss Green |
| 046 | —— | 666 | Bright Christmas Red |
| 1013 | —— | 3778 | Light Terra Cotta |
| 1076 | —— | 3847 | Dark Teal Green |

### STRAIGHT STITCH

| ANCHOR | | DMC | COLOR |
|---|---|---|---|
| 305 | —— | 728 | Topaz |
| 1076 | —— | 3847 | Dark Teal Green |
| 1070 | —— | 3849 | Light Teal Green |

### ALGERIAN EYELET

| ANCHOR | | DMC | COLOR |
|---|---|---|---|
| 1040 | ✳ | 3023 | Light Brown Gray |

*Note: Not all colors are used in each design.*

**Algerian Eyelet**

## Jolly Santa Bookmarks

### Fabric (each design)

- One 5" × 8" piece of 14-ct. Natural Brown Aida

### Design Size (each design)

- 14-ct. = 2" × 5"

### Instructions

Center the design and begin stitching. Work cross-stitches, quarter stitches, and Algerian eyelets with two strands of cotton embroidery floss. Work backstitches, straight stitches, and French knots with one strand of cotton embroidery floss. Use a pressing cloth to carefully iron the needlework from the back. Trim the needlework to within three unstitched rows. Pull out two rows of fabric threads on all sides to fringe the edges, leaving one unstitched row on all sides.

## Merry Christmas Santa Pillow

### Fabric
- One 18" × 18" piece of 28-ct. Natural Brown Linen (stitched over two threads)

### Design Size
- 28-ct. = 11¼" × 11¼"

### Finishing Materials
- ½ yard of red plaid fabric
- 14" × 14" piece of lightweight fusible interfacing
- 3 yards of decorative ribbon
- Matching sewing thread
- Polyester fiberfill

### General Instructions
Center the design and begin stitching over two fabric threads. Work cross-stitches with two strands of cotton embroidery floss. Use a pressing cloth to carefully iron the needlework from the back before finishing.

### Finishing Instructions
Use a ¼" seam allowance for all sewing unless otherwise specified. Center the interfacing on the wrong side of the needlework and, following the manufacturer's directions, fuse into place. Center and trim the needlework to 13¾" × 13¾".

Cut a 4½" × 13¾" piece of plaid fabric. Cut two 18" pieces of decorative ribbon. Working on the right side of the fabric, align the cut edges with the left long edge of the plaid fabric. Baste each ribbon in place so it is 1¾" from the center of the long edge.

Merry Christmas Santa Pillow   Stitch Count = 157w × 157h   (A)

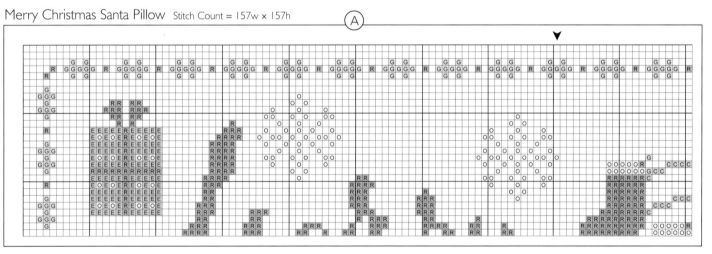

# Celebrating
# Santa

|   | A | B |
|---|---|---|
|   | C | D |

(B)

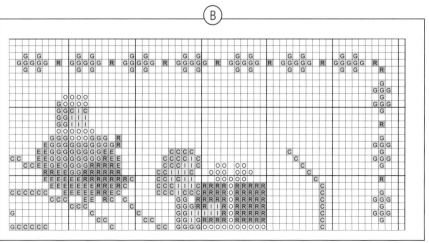

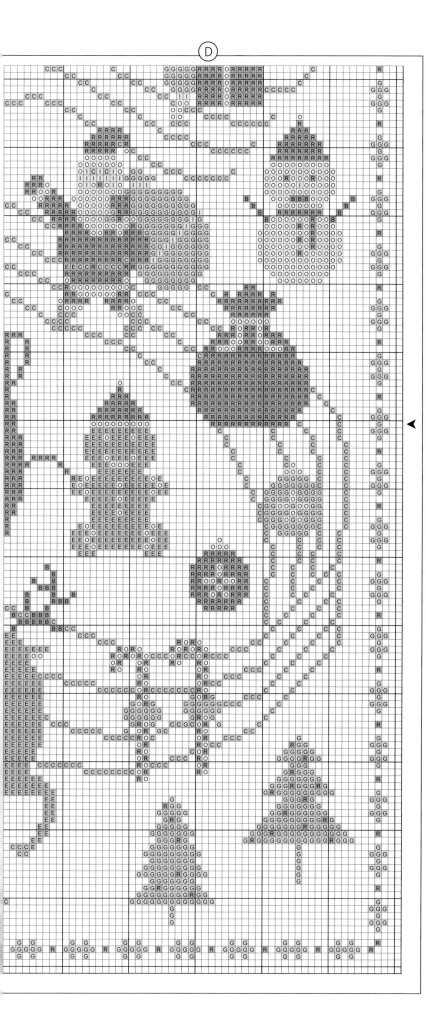

With right sides together and ribbon sandwiched in between, sew the plaid fabric to the right edge of the needlework. Press. Cut a 13¾" piece of decorative ribbon. Center the ribbon over the seam just sewn and topstitch in place.

Repeat for the pillow back, replacing the needlework section with a 13¾" × 13¾" piece of plaid fabric.

With right sides together and ribbons aligned, sew the pillow front to the pillow back, leaving an opening for turning. Make sure the ribbons do not get caught in the end seam. Trim the corners, turn, and press. Stuff with fiberfill and whipstitch the opening closed. Tie the ribbons into decorative bows.

## CROSS-STITCH

| ANCHOR | | DMC | COLOR |
|--------|---|------|-------|
| 013 | R | 349 | Dark Coral |
| 358 | B | 433 | Medium Brown |
| 901 | E | 680 | Dark Old Gold |
| 257 | G | 905 | Dark Parrot Green |
| 006 | I | 967 | Very Light Apricot |
| 905 | C | 3021 | Very Dark Brown Gray |
| 002 | O | 3865 | Winter White |

## Project Tip

**Keeping Fabric Clean in a Hoop**
When using a hoop, try putting a sheet of white tissue paper in the hoop on top of the fabric. Tear away the tissue paper in the area where you are stitching. This keeps oils from your hands from getting on the fabric and helps keep the needlework piece free from stains. And whether you use a hoop or not, always wash and dry your hands completely before starting any stitching.

Stitch Count = 114w × 140h

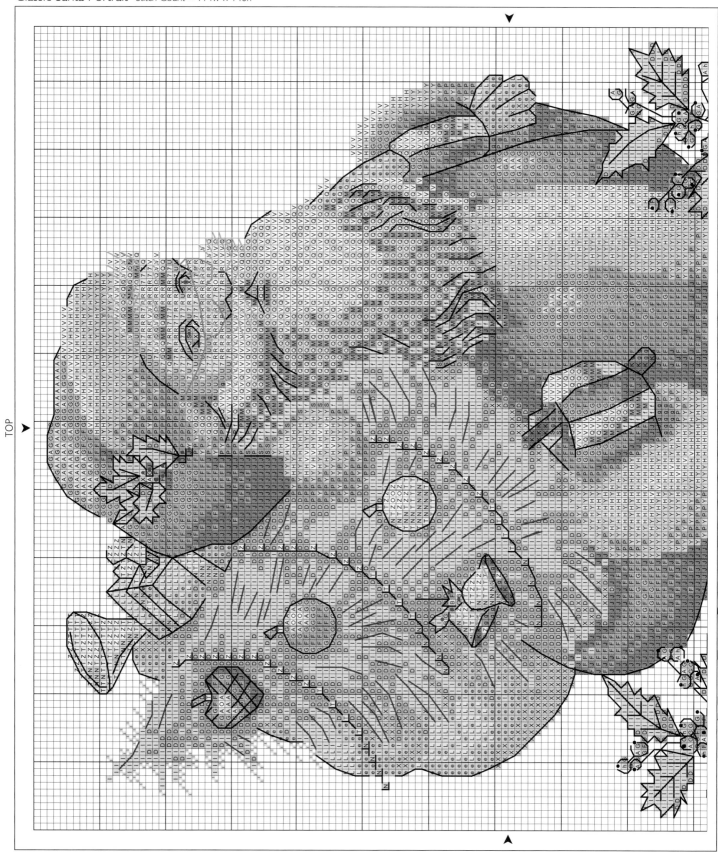

CROSS-STITCH

| ANCHOR | | DMC | COLOR |
|---|---|---|---|
| 001 | O | B5200 | Snow White |
| 403 | X | 310 | Black |
| 979 | e | 312 | Very Dark Baby Blue |

CROSS-STITCH

| ANCHOR | | DMC | COLOR |
|---|---|---|---|
| 399 | f | 318 | Light Steel Gray |
| 9046 | F | 321 | Christmas Red |
| 978 | L | 322 | Dark Baby Blue |

CROSS-STITCH

| ANCHOR | | DMC | COLOR |
|---|---|---|---|
| 235 | S | 414 | Dark Steel Gray |
| 398 | M | 415 | Pearl Gray |
| 358 | K | 433 | Medium Brown |

## Classic Santa Portrait

### Fabric
• One 16" × 18" piece
  of 28-ct. Ivory Jobelan®
  (stitched over two threads)

### Design Size
• 28-ct. = 8⅛" × 10"

### Instructions
Center the design and begin
stitching over two fabric threads.

Work cross-stitches and half
stitches with two strands of
cotton embroidery floss.
Work backstitches and French
knots with one strand of cotton
embroidery floss. Use a pressing
cloth to carefully iron the
needlework from the back
before framing as desired.

# Celebrating Santa

## CROSS-STITCH

| ANCHOR | | DMC | COLOR |
|---|---|---|---|
| 046 | G | 666 | Bright Christmas Red |
| 891 | Z | 676 | Light Old Gold |
| 890 | T | 729 | Medium Old Gold |
| 882 | U | 758 | Very Light Terra Cotta |
| 234 | Q | 762 | Very Light Pearl Gray |
| 390 | H | 822 | Light Beige Gray |
| 1044 | D | 895 | Very Dark Hunter Green |
| 1004 | b | 920 | Medium Copper |
| 1011 | R | 948 | Very Light Peach |
| 4146 | 7 | 950 | Light Desert Sand |
| 903 | P | 3032 | Medium Mocha Brown |
| 267 | I | 3346 | Hunter Green |
| 264 | B | 3348 | Light Yellow Green |
| 035 | A | 3705 | Dark Melon |
| 1037 | V | 3756 | Ultra Very Light Baby Blue |
| 901 | N | 3829 | Very Dark Old Gold |

## CROSS-STITCH

| ANCHOR | | DMC | COLOR |
|---|---|---|---|
| 1003 | C | 3853 | Dark Autumn Gold |
| 313 | h | 3854 | Medium Autumn Gold |

## FRENCH KNOT

| ANCHOR | | DMC | COLOR |
|---|---|---|---|
| 001 | • | B5200 | Snow White |
| 403 | • | 310 | Black |

## BACKSTITCH

| ANCHOR | | DMC | COLOR |
|---|---|---|---|
| 001 | — | B5200 | Winter White |
| 403 | — | 310 | Black |
| 1044 | — | 895 | Very Dark Hunter Green |
| 264 | — | 3348 | Light Yellow Green |
| 901 | — | 3829 | Very Dark Old Gold |

## CROSS-STITCH

| ANCHOR | | DMC | COLOR |
|---|---|---|---|
| 310 | g | 434 | Light Brown |
| 1005 | J | 498 | Dark Christmas Red |
| 830 | Y | 644 | Medium Beige Gray |

**Lantern Santa** Stitch Count = 40w × 41h

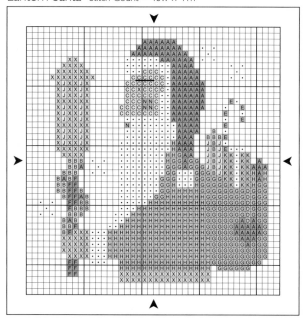

**Cardinal Santa** Stitch Count = 39w × 43h

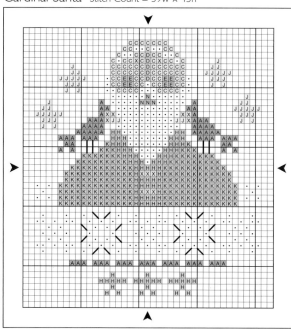

**Lollipop Santa** Stitch Count = 42w × 42h

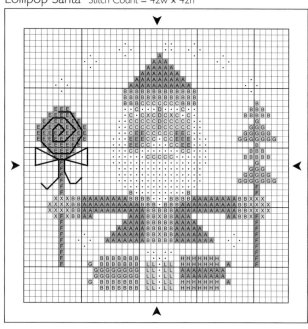

### CROSS-STITCH

| ANCHOR | | DMC | COLOR |
|---|---|---|---|
| 002 | • | White | White |
| 403 | X | 310 | Black |
| 215 | B | 320 | Medium Pistachio Green |
| 038 | E | 335 | Rose |
| 1025 | A | 347 | Very Dark Salmon |
| 392 | D | 642 | Dark Beige Gray |
| 891 | J | 676 | Light Old Gold |
| 307 | H | 783 | Medium Topaz |
| 023 | C | 818 | Baby Pink |
| 850 | K | 926 | Medium Gray Green |
| 360 | F | 3031 | Very Dark Mocha Brown |
| 262 | G | 3363 | Medium Pine Green |
| 075 | N | 3733 | Dusty Rose |
| 1036 | L | 3750 | Very Dark Antique Blue |

### BACKSTITCH

| ANCHOR | | DMC | COLOR |
|---|---|---|---|
| 403 | —— | 310 | Black |

*Note:* Not all colors are used in each design.

## Primitive Santa Tins

### Fabric (each design)
- One 11" × 11" piece of
  28-ct. Lambswool Jobelan®
  (stitched over two threads)

### Design Size
- Lantern Santa: 28-ct. = 2⅞" × 2⅞"
- Lollipop Santa: 28-ct. = 3" × 3"
- Cardinal Santa: 28-ct. = 2¾" × 3⅛"

### Finishing Materials
- Three 5"-diameter fluted tins
- Three 4¼"-diameter circles of mat board
- Three 4½" × 4½" pieces
  of cotton batting

- Basting spray
- Clear quick-dry craft glue
- Mini pom-pom trim
- Coordinating white ribbon

### General Instructions
Center the design and begin stitching over two fabric threads. Work cross-stitches with two strands of cotton embroidery floss. Work backstitches with one strand of cotton embroidery floss. Use a pressing cloth to carefully iron the needlework from the back before finishing.

### Finishing Instructions
Center and trim each design to within 2" of the stitching on all sides. Lightly spray each piece of mat board with basting spray and place glue-side down on the cotton batting. Trim batting to the edges of the board. Mount the needlework to the batting-covered boards, gluing the edges to the back. Cut a 16" length of mini pom-pom trim and glue to the edges of the needlework. Glue the wrapped needlework to the inside of the fluted tins and a ribbon hanger to the back of the tins.

## Skating Claus Snow Globe

### Fabric

• One 13" × 13" piece of 28-ct. Twilight Hand-Dyed Cashel Linen (stitched over two threads)

### Design Size

• 28-ct. = 4½" × 5¼"

### Embellishments

• 1 package of Gold #62031 frosted glass seed beads by Mill Hill®

### Finishing Materials

• Shadow box with 6¾" × 6¾" opening
• 6¾" × 6¾" piece of mat board
• ⅛" white pom-poms
• ⅜" white pom-poms
• Clear quick-dry craft glue

### General Instructions

Center the design and begin stitching over two fabric threads. Work cross-stitches, half stitches, and quarter stitches with two strands of cotton embroidery floss. Work backstitches and French knots with one strand of cotton embroidery floss. Attach beads with one strand of coordinating floss. Lay the needlework facedown on a terry cloth towel (to protect beads) and use a pressing cloth to carefully iron the needlework from the back before finishing.

### Finishing Instructions

Center and trim the needlework to within 2" of the stitching on the sides and bottom and 1½" on the top. Mount the needlework on a piece of mat board, with approximately 1½" between the bottom of the stitching and the bottom of the mat board and centering horizontally. Glue the edges of the fabric to the back.

Insert the needlework into the back of the shadowbox. Glue pom-poms along the bottom of the needlework fabric to create a snow pile.

## Celebrating Santa

### CROSS-STITCH

| ANCHOR | | DMC | COLOR |
|---|---|---|---|
| 001 | O | B5200 | Snow White |
| 403 | X | 310 | Black |
| 1017 | P | 316 | Medium Antique Mauve |
| 374 | J | 420 | Dark Hazelnut Brown |
| 212 | E | 561 | Very Dark Jade |
| 891 | C | 676 | Light Old Gold |
| 1012 | Z | 754 | Light Peach |
| 234 | H | 762 | Very Light Pearl Gray |
| 045 | V | 814 | Dark Garnet |
| 1005 | S | 816 | Garnet |
| 9159 | N | 828 | Ultra Very Light Blue |
| 944 | L | 869 | Very Dark Hazelnut Brown |
| 1011 | T | 948 | Very Light Peach |

### FRENCH KNOT

| ANCHOR | | DMC | COLOR |
|---|---|---|---|
| 403 | • | 310 | Black |

### STRAIGHT STITCH

| ANCHOR | | DMC | COLOR |
|---|---|---|---|
| 001 | —— | B5200 | Snow White |
| 403 | —— | 310 | Black |
| 891 | —— | 676 | Light Old Gold |
| 923 | —— | 699 | Christmas Green |
| 234 | —— | 762 | Very Light Pearl Gray |
| 045 | —— | 814 | Dark Garnet |
| 9159 | —— | 828 | Ultra Very Light Blue |
| 1011 | —— | 948 | Very Light Peach |

### BEAD

| MILL HILL FROSTED GLASS SEED | COLOR |
|---|---|
| 62031 | Gold |

# Playful
# Palette

*Get crafty this holiday season with a DIY-inspired collection of Christmas cross-stitch.*

Bright splashes of color come together in imaginative, patchwork designs that give off a cheerful, exuberant energy to fill the holidays. Kick off your seasonal stitching with Cheryl McKinnon's trendy hoop collage filled with fun details, or roll up your sleeves with a sparkling bird snow globe, a set of sassy sweaters, or a topsy-turvy car expertly packed for the drive home. No matter which you choose, you're sure to create a finished piece bursting with handmade charm.

**Project instructions begin on page 32.**

*The fabulous poses and updated vintage styling of these "ugly sweaters"* designed by Alyssa Westhoek will have your home filled with admiring giggles. Hanging on the tree or atop a craft-paper present, their style will shine through.

**Project instructions begin on page 34.**

# Playful **Palette**

*Set in her own snowy scene, this girly polar bear* designed by Barbara Ana is quite the statement piece. Clever detailing adds realism to the glass cloche and fuzzy fur while crafty stars and snow keep the design whimsical.

**Project instructions begin on page 36.**

# Playful
# Palette

*You'll love the vibrant patterns and colors in this one-reindeer sleigh* designed by Barbara Sestok. This handsome lad is all decked out and ready to deliver wonderful Christmas presents to the world's children.

**Project instructions begin on page 38.**

*Feather your nest for the holidays like this spectacular little bird in her 3D home!* Design team Praiseworthy Stitches incorporated a craft ornament, artificial snow, tinsel, and metallic threads to achieve this special ornament.

**Project instructions begin on page 40.**

*Just like the song itself, this bold typographical pattern* esigned by Kathleen Berlew is filled with effortless Christmas cheer. An eye-catching gradient pattern and a modern font will make this simple artwork shine!

**Project instructions begin on page 41.**

# Playful Palette

*A perfect project for your holiday travels, this colorful car infuses* those sometimes-hectic plans with fun and whimsy. Designed by Emma Congdon, this little car is sure to deliver a ton of joy to your Christmas stitching.

**Project instructions begin on page 42.**

A Very Merry Christmas Stitch Count = 116w × 116h

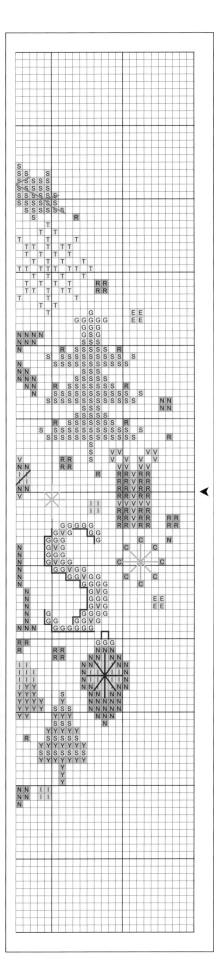

## A Very Merry Christmas

### Fabric

- One 16" × 16" piece of 28-ct. White Cashel (stitched over two threads)

### Design Size

- 28-ct. = 8¼" × 8¼"

### Finishing Materials

- ¼ yard coordinating print fabric
- 9" embroidery hoop
- Clear quick-dry craft glue

### General Instructions

Center the design and begin stitching over two fabric threads. Work cross-stitches with two strands of cotton embroidery floss. Work backstitches with one strand of cotton embroidery floss. Use a pressing cloth to carefully iron the needlework from the back before finishing.

### Finishing Instructions

Cut ¾" strips of coordinating print fabric. Glue one end to the inside edge of the outer embroidery hoop. Wrap the strip around the hoop, overlapping slightly to cover the entire hoop. Glue the end in place. Continue with new strips until the hoop is covered.

Insert the needlework into the wrapped hoop. Trim the excess needlework fabric to 1" and stitch a running stitch ¼" from the edge. Pull the running stitch tight on the back and tie the ends.

# Playful
# Palette

## Project Tip

### Changing Design Size

Most cross-stitch designs can be adapted to different sizes just by changing the thread count of the fabric. To determine the final design size when stitched on a different count of fabric, just divide the stitch count by the thread count. Remember to use half of the thread count when stitching over two threads.

### CROSS-STITCH

| ANCHOR | | DMC | COLOR |
|---|---|---|---|
| 055 | I | 604 | Light Cranberry |
| 046 | R | 666 | Bright Christmas Red |
| 088 | N | 718 | Plum |
| 295 | G | 726 | Light Topaz |
| 257 | Y | 905 | Dark Parrot Green |
| 255 | S | 907 | Light Parrot Green |
| 186 | V | 959 | Medium Sea Green |
| 185 | T | 964 | Light Sea Green |
| 085 | E | 3609 | Ultra Light Plum |
| 188 | C | 3812 | Very Dark Sea Green |

### BACKSTITCH

| ANCHOR | | DMC | COLOR |
|---|---|---|---|
| 055 | —— | 604 | Light Cranberry |
| 046 | —— | 666 | Bright Christmas Red |
| 088 | —— | 718 | Plum |
| 295 | —— | 726 | Light Topaz |
| 257 | —— | 905 | Dark Parrot Green |
| 188 | —— | 3812 | Very Dark Sea Green |

## Tree Turtleneck  Stitch Count = 55w × 48h

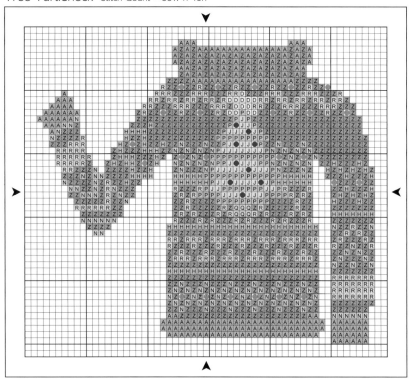

## Holiday Turtlenecks

### Fabric (each design)

- One 8" × 8" piece of 14-ct. Antique Brown Perforated Paper

### Design Size

- Tree Turtleneck: 14-ct. = 3⅞" × 3⅜"
- Bow Turtleneck: 14-ct. = 3⅞" × 3⅜"
- Snowman Turtleneck: 14-ct. = 4⅞" × 3⅜"
- Poinsettia Turtleneck: 14-ct. = 3⅜" × 3½"
- Reindeer Turtleneck: 14-ct. = 3¼" × 3½"

### Embellishments

- 1 package each of Old Rose #00553, Old Gold #00557, and Ice #02010 glass seed beads by Mill Hill®
- 1 package each of Abalone #03037 and Cinnamon Red #03048 antique glass seed beads by Mill Hill

### Finishing Materials

- Coordinating twine

### Instructions

Center the design and begin stitching. Work cross-stitches with two strands of cotton embroidery floss. Attach beads with one strand of coordinating floss. Trim the finished needlework to within one unstitched row on all sides. Affix a piece of coordinating twine to the back for a hanger.

## Bow Turtleneck  Stitch Count = 55w × 47h

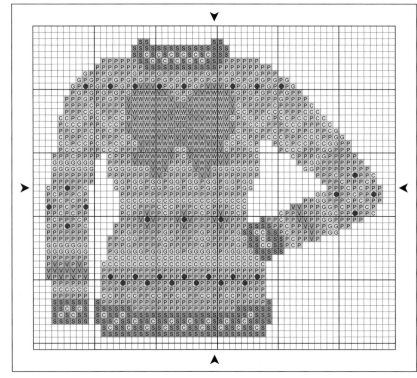

## Project Tip

### Stitching on Perforated Paper

When stitching on perforated paper, be careful not to pull the thread too tightly, as it can break through and tear the paper. Do not drag threads over open areas, as they will be more visible than on aida or linen. Also, perforated paper cannot be ironed or washed, so take care to prevent wrinkles and smudges as you stitch.

## CROSS-STITCH

| ANCHOR | | DMC | COLOR |
|---|---|---|---|
| 002 | • | White | White |
| 175 | K | 160 | Medium Gray Blue |
| 403 | X | 310 | Black |
| 013 | V | 349 | Dark Coral |
| 217 | P | 367 | Dark Pistachio Green |
| 943 | Q | 422 | Light Hazelnut Brown |
| 227 | J | 701 | Light Christmas Green |
| 256 | G | 704 | Bright Chartreuse |
| 300 | D | 745 | Light Pale Yellow |
| 968 | U | 778 | Very Light Antique Mauve |
| 035 | W | 891 | Dark Carnation |
| 089 | A | 917 | Medium Plum |
| 1035 | M | 930 | Dark Antique Blue |
| 152 | L | 939 | Very Dark Navy Blue |
| 073 | N | 963 | Ultra Very Light Dusty Rose |
| 246 | S | 986 | Very Dark Forest Green |
| 187 | C | 992 | Medium Aquamarine |
| 329 | Y | 3340 | Medium Apricot |
| 087 | Z | 3607 | Light Plum |
| 066 | T | 3688 | Light Mauve |
| 062 | B | 3805 | Cyclamen Pink |
| 066 | H | 3806 | Light Cyclamen Pink |
| 188 | R | 3812 | Very Dark Sea Green |

### Snowman Turtleneck  Stitch Count = 68w × 47h

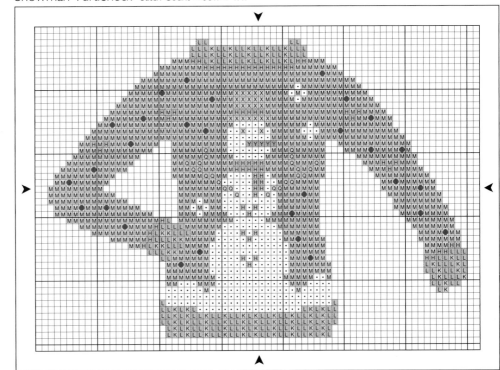

### BEAD

| MILL HILL GLASS SEED | | COLOR |
|---|---|---|
| 00553 | ● | Old Rose |
| 00557 | ○ | Old Gold |
| 02010 | ● | Ice |

### BEAD

| MILL HILL ANTIQUE GLASS SEED | | COLOR |
|---|---|---|
| 03037 | ● | Abalone |
| 03048 | ● | Cinnamon Red |

*Note:* Not all colors are used in each design.

# Playful Palette

### Poinsettia Turtleneck  Stitch Count = 47w × 49h

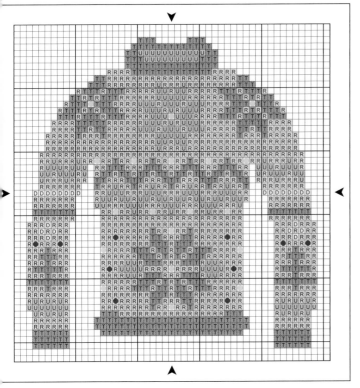

### Reindeer Turtleneck  Stitch Count = 45w × 50h

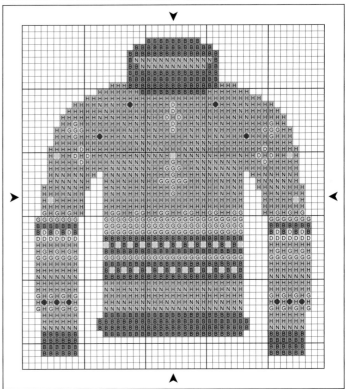

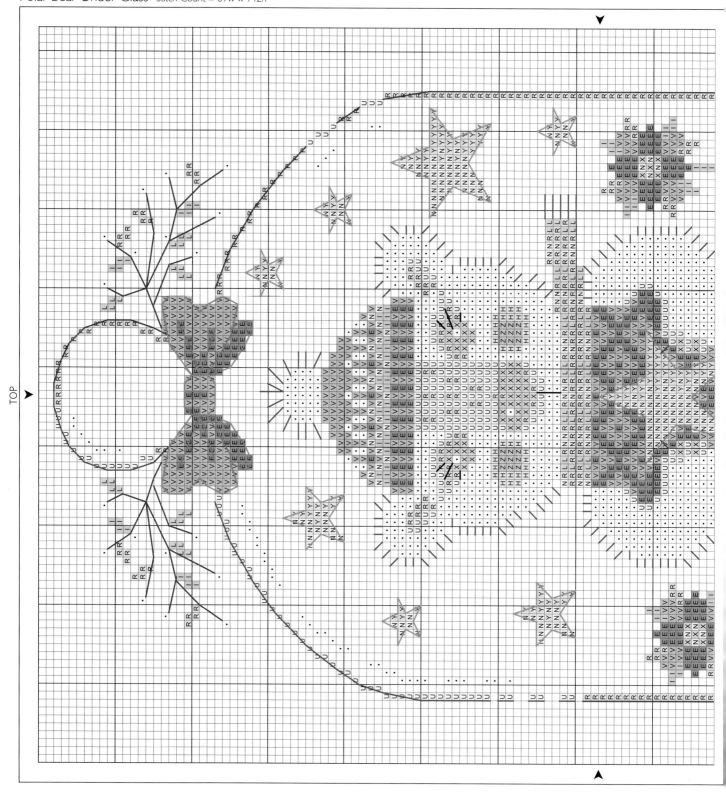

## Polar Bear Under Glass

### Fabric
• One 14" × 18" piece of 14-ct. Tropical Green Aida

### Design Size
• 14-ct. = 6⅜" × 10⅛"

### Instructions
Center the design and begin stitching. Work cross-stitches, quarter stitches, and DMC® 726/Anchor 295 backstitches with two strands of cotton embroidery floss. Work remaining backstitches with one strand of cotton embroidery floss. Use a pressing cloth to carefully iron the needlework from the back before framing as desired.

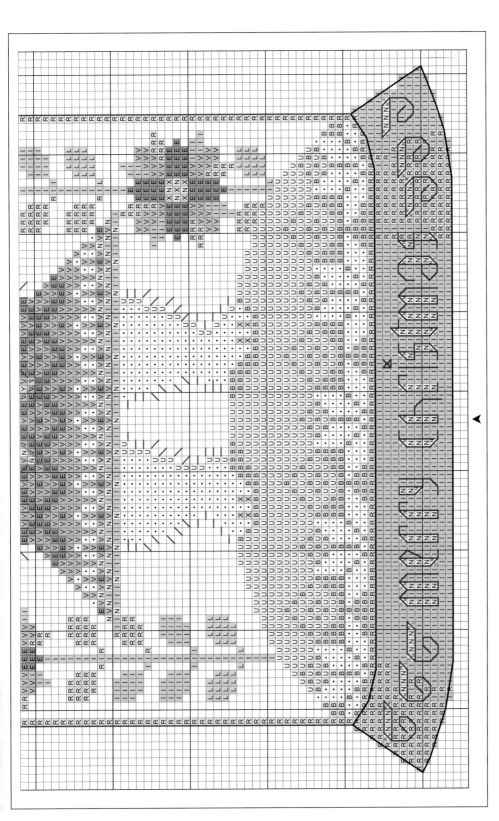

# Playful
# Palette

## CROSS-STITCH

| ANCHOR | | DMC | COLOR |
|---|---|---|---|
| 001 | · | B5200 | Snow White |
| 403 | X | 310 | Black |
| 098 | L | 553 | Violet |
| 295 | N | 726 | Light Topaz |
| 303 | Y | 742 | Light Tangerine |
| 158 | U | 747 | Very Light Sky Blue |
| 023 | Z | 818 | Baby Pink |
| 271 | H | 819 | Light Baby Pink |
| 433 | R | 996 | Medium Electric Blue |
| 063 | E | 3804 | Dark Cyclamen Pink |
| 066 | V | 3806 | Light Cyclamen Pink |
| 928 | B | 3811 | Very Light Turquoise |
| 1089 | I | 3843 | Electric Blue |

## BACKSTITCH

| ANCHOR | | DMC | COLOR |
|---|---|---|---|
| 001 | —— | B5200 | Snow White |
| 403 | —— | 310 | Black |
| 295 | —— | 726 | Light Topaz |
| 309 | —— | 780 | Ultra Very Dark Topaz |
| 1089 | —— | 3843 | Electric Blue |

## Project Tip

### Going With the Grain

By following the grain of embroidery floss, you lessen the wear and tear on your thread as you draw it through the fabric. To find the grain direction, cut a length of floss. Loop the thread over so both the cut ends lie next to each other. Do not allow the two ends to bundle together, as you must be able to differentiate between them. Holding the cut lengths close together, about ½" from the tips, use one finger of your free hand to gently tap the cut ends. Watch carefully—the end that balloons most is the end that should be threaded through your needle (and is the shorter tail).

## Season's Greetings Sleigh

### Fabric
- One 17" × 16" piece of 28-ct. Wood Violet Jobelan®
  (stitched over two threads)

### Design Size
- 28-ct. = 9¼" × 7⅞"

### Instructions
Center the design and begin stitching over two fabric threads.
Work cross-stitches and quarter stitches with two strands of
cotton embroidery floss. Work straight stitches and French
knots with one strand of cotton embroidery floss or DMC®
Light Effects floss. Use a pressing cloth to carefully iron
the needlework from the back before framing as desired.

# Playful Palette

CROSS-STITCH

| ANCHOR | | DMC | COLOR |
|---|---|---|---|
| 002 | · | White | White |
| 1046 | T | 435 | Very Light Brown |
| 266 | F | 470 | Light Avocado Green |
| 167 | D | 598 | Light Turquoise |
| 305 | E | 728 | Topaz |
| 275 | R | 746 | Off White |
| 089 | B | 917 | Medium Plum |
| 269 | J | 936 | Very Dark Avocado Green |
| 316 | G | 970 | Light Pumpkin |
| 087 | A | 3607 | Light Plum |
| 049 | N | 3689 | Very Light Mauve |
| 236 | X | 3799 | Very Dark Pewter Gray |
| 168 | C | 3810 | Dark Turquoise |
| 305 | H | 3821 | Straw |

FRENCH KNOT

| ANCHOR | | DMC | COLOR |
|---|---|---|---|
| 002 | ● | White | White |
| 305 | ● | 728 | Topaz |
| 316 | ● | 970 | Light Pumpkin |
| 049 | ● | 3689 | Very Light Mauve |

STRAIGHT STITCH

| ANCHOR | DMC | COLOR |
|---|---|---|
| 002 | White | White |
| 305 | 728 | Topaz |
| 089 | 917 | Medium Plum |
| 269 | 936 | Very Dark Avocado Green |
| 316 | 970 | Light Pumpkin |
| 236 | 3799 | Very Dark Pewter Gray |
| 168 | 3810 | Dark Turquoise |

| DMC LIGHT EFFECTS | COLOR |
|---|---|
| E415 | Silver |

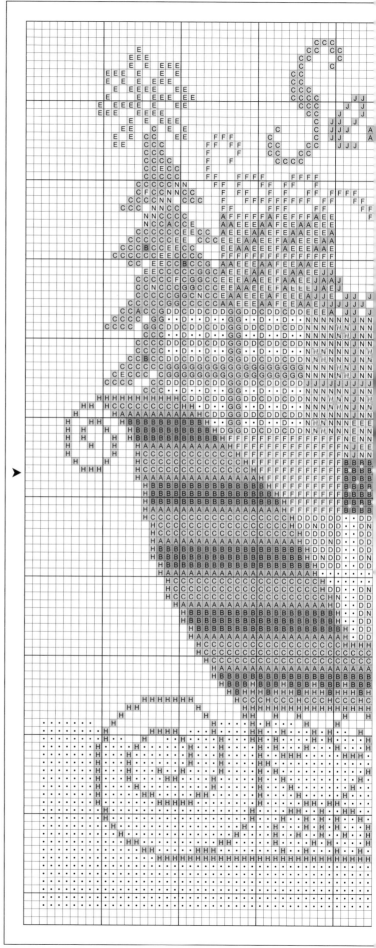

TOP

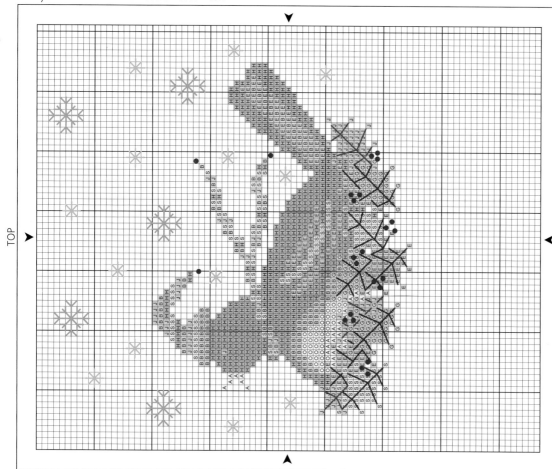

## CROSS-STITCH

| WEEKS DYE WORKS | | COLOR |
|---|---|---|
| 1091 | O | Whitewash |
| GENTLE ARTS SAMPLER | | COLOR |
| 0910 | E | Peacock |

## CROSS-STITCH WITH BLENDED THREAD

| WEEKS DYE WORKS | | COLOR |
|---|---|---|
| 1334 | H | Merlot |
| KREINIK BLENDING FILAMENT | | COLOR |
| 031 | | Crimson |
| GENTLE ARTS SHAKER | | COLOR |
| 7010 | A | Ohio Lemon |
| KREINIK BLENDING FILAMENT | | COLOR |
| 091 | | Star Yellow |
| GENTLE ARTS SAMPLER | | COLOR |
| 0920 | S | Tropical Ocean |
| KREINIK BLENDING FILAMENT | | COLOR |
| 094 | | Star Blue |
| GENTLE ARTS SHAKER | | COLOR |
| 7080 | G | Endive |
| KREINIK BLENDING FILAMENT | | COLOR |
| 085 | | Peacock |
| WEEKS DYE WORKS | | COLOR |
| 3960 | J | Teal Frost |
| KREINIK BLENDING FILAMENT | | COLOR |
| 009 | | Emerald |
| GENTLE ARTS SHAKER | | COLOR |
| 7035 | B | Tea Rose |
| KREINIK BLENDING FILAMENT | | COLOR |
| 092 | | Star Pink |

## BACKSTITCH

| GENTLE ARTS SAMPLER | | COLOR |
|---|---|---|
| 0910 | — | Peacock |
| WEEKS DYE WORKS | | COLOR |
| 1091 | — | Whitewash |
| WEEKS DYE WORKS | | COLOR |
| 3960 | — | Teal Frost |

## SMYRNA CROSS

| WEEKS DYE WORKS | | COLOR |
|---|---|---|
| 1091 | ✳ | Whitewash |

## BEAD

| MILL HILL PETITE GLASS SEED | COLOR |
|---|---|
| 42043 ● | Rich Red |

**Smyrna Cross**

## Holly Bird Globe

### Fabric
• One 11" × 14" piece of 32-ct. Vintage Winter Sky Hand-Dyed Linen (stitched over two threads)

### Design Size
• 32-ct. = 4⅛" × 4"

### Embellishments
• 1 package of Rich Red #42043 petite glass seed beads by Mill Hill®

### Finishing Materials
• One half of 5" snap-on plastic ornament
• Two 6" × 6" pieces of foam board
• Quilt batting
• Clear quick dry craft glue
• Artificial snow
• 12" length of tinsel trim
• Coordinating ribbon
• One 5" × 5" piece of white felt

### General Instructions
Center the design, including the 20 blank rows at the bottom of the chart, and begin stitching over two fabric threads. Work cross-stitches with 2 strands of Weeks Dye Works floss or Gentle Arts Sampler thread. Work blended cross-stitches with 2 strands of Weeks Dye Works floss or Gentle Arts Shaker or Sampler thread and 1 strand of Kreinik blending filament. Work snowflake backstitches and Smyrna crosses with 2 strands of Weeks Dye Works floss. Work remaining backstitches with one strand of Weeks Dye Works floss or Gentle Arts Sampler thread. To maximize color changes when stitching with hand-dyed floss, complete each cross-stitch before moving on to the next one. Attach beads with one strand of coordinating floss. Lay the needlework facedown on a terry cloth towel (to protect beads)

and use a pressing cloth to carefully iron the needlework from the back before finishing.

### Finishing Instructions
Cut one piece of foam board into a 4¾" circle. Layer quilt batting over the foam circle. Layer the stitched needlework over the batting, slightly above center so there is room for snow at the bottom. Affix the edges of the fabric to the back.

Cut the remaining piece of foam board into a 5¼" circle. Glue the mounted needlework to the center of the larger foam circle.

Put artificial snow in the ornament half. Place a bead of glue around the edge of the ornament half and fit over the top of the stitched design. Let dry.

Place another bead of glue around the seam of the ornament and cover with tinsel trim.

Glue a coordinating ribbon hanger to the back and cover with felt.

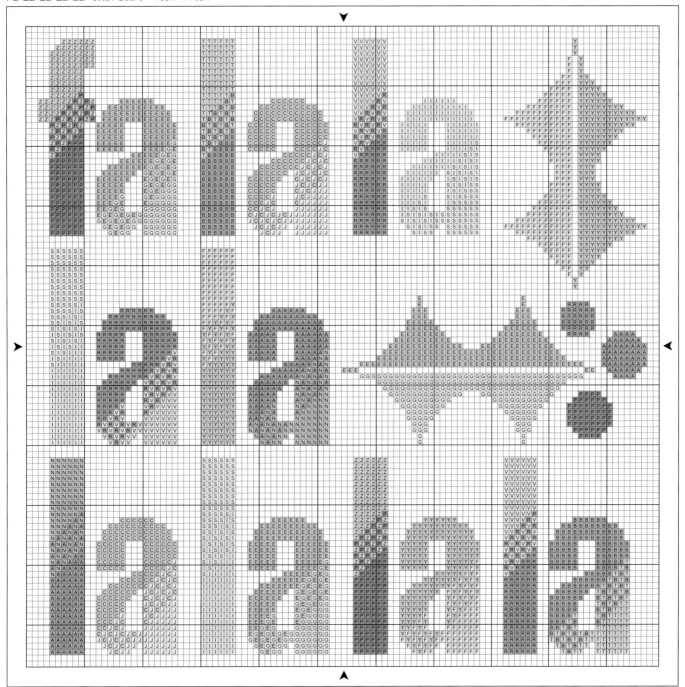

# Fa La La La La

## Fabric

- One 15" × 15" piece of 14-ct. Navy Aida

## Design Size

- 14-ct. = 7½" × 7⅜"

## Finishing Materials

- 10" × 10" artist canvas
- Spray adhesive
- Twelve ⁷⁄₁₆" decorative nails
- Twenty-eight ⅜" decorative tacks in coordinating colors

## General Instructions

Center the design and begin stitching. Work cross-stitches with two strands of cotton embroidery floss. Use a pressing cloth to carefully iron the needlework from the back before finishing.

## Finishing Instructions

Following the manufacturer's instruction, use spray adhesive to center and affix the needlework to the artist canvas. Allow to dry. Pull the fabric taut at the corner, neatly fold the fabric to left or right side of the canvas, and then to the back. Tack in place with two or three evenly spaced decorative nails on the back. Repeat with each corner and trim the excess fabric. Evenly space seven colored tacks on each side edge of the canvas.

## CROSS-STITCH

| ANCHOR | | DMC | COLOR |
|---|---|---|---|
| 110 | B | 208 | Very Dark Lavender |
| 108 | T | 210 | Medium Lavender |
| 253 | J | 472 | Ultra Light Avocado Green |
| 206 | F | 564 | Very Light Jade |
| 062 | R | 603 | Cranberry |
| 050 | V | 605 | Very Light Cranberry |
| 088 | A | 718 | Plum |
| 293 | S | 727 | Very Light Topaz |
| 305 | I | 728 | Topaz |
| 255 | C | 907 | Light Parrot Green |
| 209 | Y | 912 | Light Emerald Green |
| 187 | E | 958 | Dark Sea Green |
| 185 | G | 964 | Light Sea Green |
| 085 | Z | 3609 | Ultra Light Plum |
| 063 | P | 3804 | Dark Cyclamen Pink |
| 062 | N | 3805 | Cyclamen Pink |

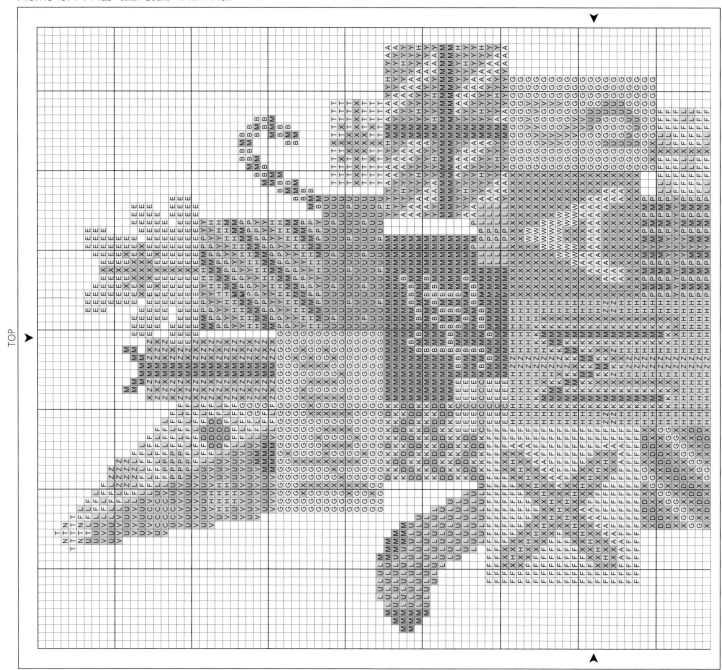

## Home for X-Mas

### Fabric
- One 13" × 18" piece of 14-ct. White Aida

### Design Size
- 14-ct. = 5¼" × 10"

### Finishing Materials
- ½ yard of red print fabric
- 7½" × 12" piece of fusible interfacing
- Matching sewing thread

### General Instructions
Center the design and begin stitching. Work cross-stitches with two strands of cotton embroidery floss. Use a pressing cloth to carefully iron the needlework from the back before finishing.

### Finishing Instructions
Use a ¼" seam allowance for all sewing unless specified. Center and trim the needlework to 7" × 11½". Center the interfacing on the wrong side of the needlework and, following the manufacturer's instructions, fuse into place.

Cut a ¾" × 7" piece of red print fabric. With right sides together, sew to the top edge of the needlework. Cut two ¾" × 11½" pieces of red print fabric. With right sides together, sew to each side edge of the needlework. Leave the bottom edge unsewn.

Cut a piece of red print fabric the same size as the front. Cut three 3½" × 2" pieces of red print fabric. Fold in half lengthwise with right sides together. Sew along the long edge and turn. Bring the short ends together, and with raw edges aligned, baste one hanger centered on the top edge of the needlework and the others 2" to either side.

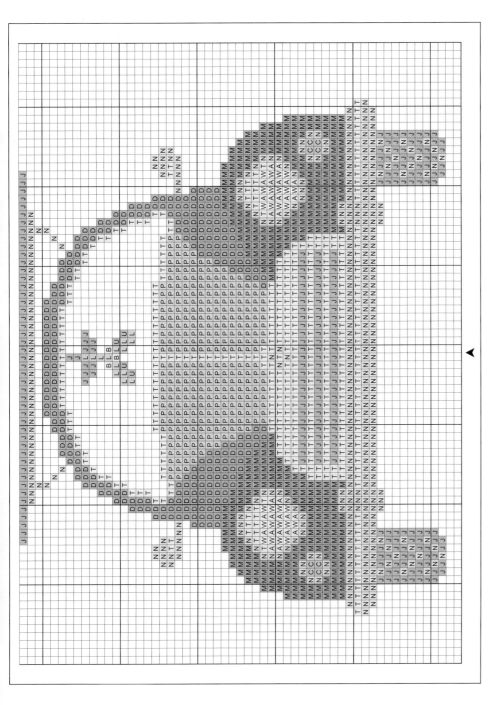

## Project Tip

**Working With Several Floss Colors**

When working with frequent color
changes, use several needles to
avoid rethreading the same needle
over and over. Work a few stitches
in one color, bring the needle to the
front of the fabric and put it aside.
Introduce the next floss color and
needle and continue.

### CROSS-STITCH

| ANCHOR | | DMC | COLOR |
|---|---|---|---|
| 235 | N | 004 | Dark Tin |
| 979 | X | 312 | Very Dark Baby Blue |
| 010 | M | 351 | Coral |
| 401 | J | 413 | Dark Pewter Gray |
| 943 | E | 422 | Light Hazelnut Brown |
| 099 | Y | 552 | Medium Violet |
| 062 | D | 603 | Cranberry |
| 055 | P | 604 | Light Cranberry |
| 050 | K | 605 | Very Light Cranberry |
| 923 | U | 699 | Christmas Green |
| 228 | V | 700 | Bright Christmas Green |
| 226 | L | 702 | Kelly Green |
| 256 | F | 704 | Bright Chartreuse |
| 316 | C | 740 | Tangerine |
| 158 | A | 747 | Very Light Sky Blue |
| 023 | B | 818 | Baby Pink |
| 274 | T | 928 | Very Light Gray Green |
| 185 | G | 964 | Light Sea Green |
| 1037 | W | 3756 | Ultra Very Light Baby Blue |
| 176 | Z | 3839 | Medium Lavender Blue |
| 1090 | H | 3846 | Light Bright Turquoise |

With right sides together, sew the front
to the back, leaving the bottom edge open
and sandwiching the hangers between.
Turn and press, folding the bottom edge
¼" to the inside. Cut four 4" × 2½" pieces
of red print fabric. Press one long edge ¼"
to the wrong side. With wrong side facing
and the pressed edge on the bottom, fold
the bottom left corner so the left raw
edge is aligned with the top edge. Repeat
with the bottom right corner, forming a
point. Press. Fold the left and right points
of the triangle ¾" to center, keeping the

top edge aligned, and press. Overlap
the finished points so the top edge
is aligned and the total width is 7".
Baste together. With folded seams
toward the back, tuck the top edge
of the points in the open bottom
of the banner. Top stitch across.

## Playful Palette

# Olive & Merlot

*Immerse yourself in the classic holiday carols, rich colors, and moments of togetherness* that come with years of treasured Christmas traditions. Familiar motifs and themes come wrapped in deep reds and natural greens in this timeless collection of hand-stitched décor.

Fill your Christmas tree with these petite winter treasures designed by Barbara Sestok or decorate your mantel with free-standing firs, a choir of caroling kitties, or a joyful portrait of a Victorian mother and child. Each piece is sure to stir up memories of Christmas past and be passed on long into Christmases yet to come.

**Project instructions begin on page 58.**

*Sprigs of pine and flowing red ribbon create a lovely hooped frame* for a classic Christmas greeting. Faby Reilly's use of metallic floss and variegated stitches bring this charming piece to life.

**Project instructions begin on page 61.**

# Olive & Merlot

*Feel the joy of Christmastime passed down through generations* in this emotive portrait designed by Elizabeth Spurlock. The addition of gold beads and a hand-dyed fabric lend this portrait true vintage flair.

**Project instructions begin on page 56.**

*All you need are two charts and three color palettes to plant a forest of 3D Christmas trees* designed by Shannan Grierson. These double-sided trees of perforated plastic are a centerpiece that looks great from every angle.

**Project instructions begin on page 54.**

*Join a trio of festive felines as they carol door-to-door* in this design by Leslie Warren. Fully stitched, this picture and "MEOW"-covered matting are a truly impressive piece of cross-stitch.

**Project instructions begin on page 62.**

# Olive & Merlot

# Olive &
# Merlot

*The bright feathers of these magnificent songbirds* mean they are always dressed up for the holidays! Designed by Julia Lucas, the three tweeters make a wonderful bell pull of diamonds on the point.

**Project instructions begin on page 51.**

Robin Stitch Count = 98w × 98h

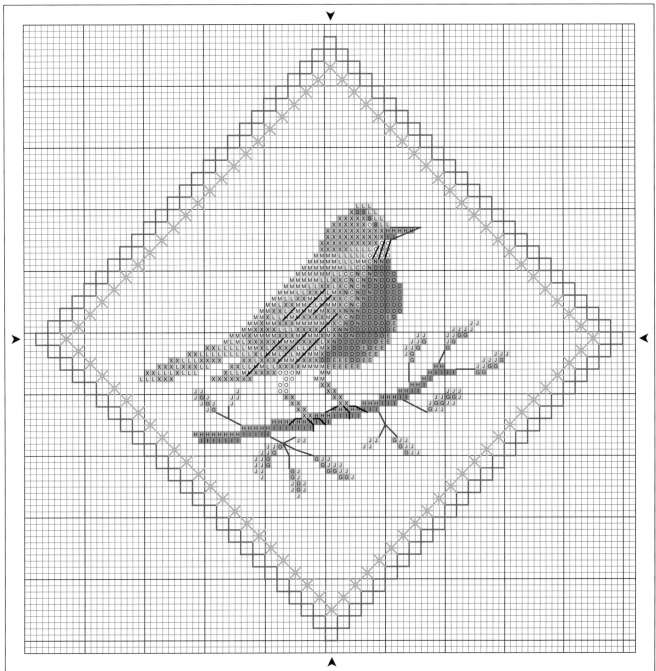

## Crimson Birds

### Fabric (each design)
- One 14" × 14" piece of 32-ct. Soft Cream Belfast® Linen (stitched over two threads)

### Design Size (each design)
- 32-ct. = 6⅛" × 6⅛"

### Finishing Materials
- ½ yard of green print fabric
- ½ yard of lightweight, fusible interfacing
- Coordinating ribbon
- Fabric glue
- Matching sewing thread

CROSS-STITCH

| ANCHOR | | DMC | COLOR |
|---|---|---|---|
| 001 | O | B5200 | Snow White |
| 403 | X | 310 | Black |
| 400 | L | 317 | Pewter Gray |
| 399 | M | 318 | Light Steel Gray |
| 013 | N | 349 | Dark Coral |
| 011 | C | 350 | Medium Coral |
| 358 | I | 433 | Medium Brown |
| 1046 | H | 435 | Very Light Brown |
| 043 | E | 815 | Medium Garnet |
| 013 | D | 817 | Very Dark Coral Red |
| 681 | G | 3051 | Dark Green Gray |
| 261 | J | 3053 | Green Gray |

CROSS-STITCH WITH BLENDED THREAD

| ANCHOR | | DMC | COLOR |
|---|---|---|---|
| 403 | S | 310 | Black |
| 400 | | 317 | Pewter Gray |

BACKSTITCH

| ANCHOR | | DMC | COLOR |
|---|---|---|---|
| 001 | —— | B5200 | Snow White |
| 403 | —— | 310 | Black |
| 358 | —— | 433 | Medium Brown |

FOUR-SIDED STITCH

| ANCHOR | | DMC | COLOR |
|---|---|---|---|
| 043 | □ | 815 | Medium Garnet |

ALGERIAN EYELET

| ANCHOR | | DMC | COLOR |
|---|---|---|---|
| 261 | ✳ | 3053 | Green Gray |

*Note:* Not all colors are used in each design.

**Cardinal** Stitch Count = 98w × 98h

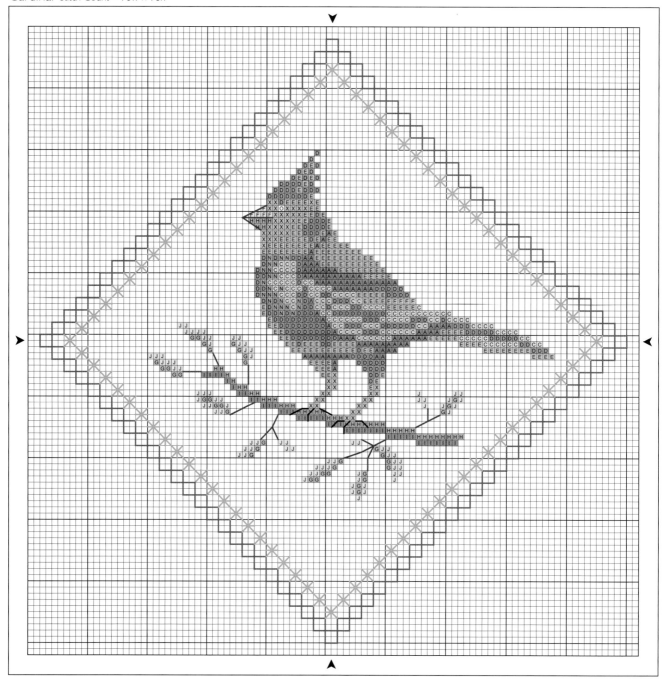

**General Instructions**

Center the design and begin stitching over two fabric threads. Work cross-stitches, Algerian eyelets, and four-sided stitches with two strands of cotton embroidery floss. Work backstitches with one strand of cotton embroidery floss. Use a pressing cloth to carefully iron the needlework from the back before finishing.

**Finishing Instructions**

Use a ¼" seam allowance for all sewing unless otherwise specified. Center the interfacing on the wrong side of the needlework and, following the manufacturer's directions, fuse into place. Center and trim the needlework to within ½" of the needlework on each edge.

Using the trimmed needlework as a guide, cut three diamonds from the green print fabric. With wrong sides facing, baste the front and back pieces together along the outer row of stitching on all sides.

Cut three 27" × 3" green print fabric strips. Fold the strips in half lengthwise with the wrong sides together to create a binding. With right sides together and the cut binding edges ¼" from the edge of the stitching, sew the binding piece around each ornament, folding to form a miter at each corner. Press the binding to the back and hand-stitch into place.

Cut a 24" piece of coordinating ribbon. Arrange the finished needlework pieces vertically on the ribbon and glue into place with fabric glue. Embellish and hang as desired.

## Scarlet Tanager Stitch Count = 98w × 98h

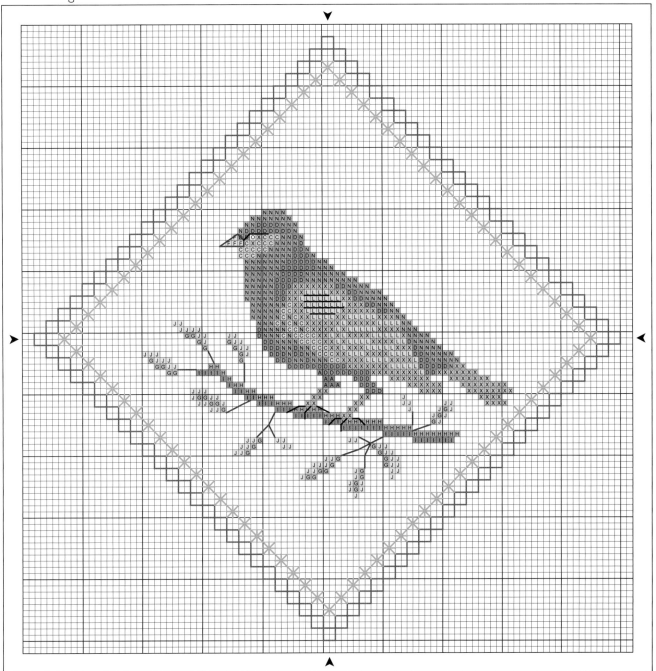

### CROSS-STITCH

| ANCHOR | | DMC | COLOR |
|---|---|---|---|
| 001 | O | B5200 | Snow White |
| 403 | X | 310 | Black |
| 400 | L | 317 | Pewter Gray |
| 399 | M | 318 | Light Steel Gray |
| 013 | N | 349 | Dark Coral |
| 011 | C | 350 | Medium Coral |
| 358 | I | 433 | Medium Brown |
| 1046 | H | 435 | Very Light Brown |
| 362 | F | 437 | Light Tan |
| 043 | E | 815 | Medium Garnet |
| 013 | D | 817 | Very Dark Coral Red |
| 897 | A | 902 | Very Dark Garnet |
| 681 | G | 3051 | Dark Green Gray |
| 261 | J | 3053 | Green Gray |

### CROSS-STITCH WITH BLENDED THREAD

| ANCHOR | | DMC | COLOR |
|---|---|---|---|
| 403 | S | 310 | Black |
| 400 | | 317 | Pewter Gray |

### BACKSTITCH

| ANCHOR | | DMC | COLOR |
|---|---|---|---|
| 001 | —— | B5200 | Snow White |
| 403 | —— | 310 | Black |
| 358 | —— | 433 | Medium Brown |

### FOUR-SIDED STITCH

| ANCHOR | | DMC | COLOR |
|---|---|---|---|
| 043 | □ | 815 | Medium Garnet |

### ALGERIAN EYELET

| ANCHOR | | DMC | COLOR |
|---|---|---|---|
| 261 | ✳ | 3053 | Green Gray |

*Note:* Not all colors
are used in each design.

Olive &
Merlot

Four-Sided Stitch

Algerian Eyelet

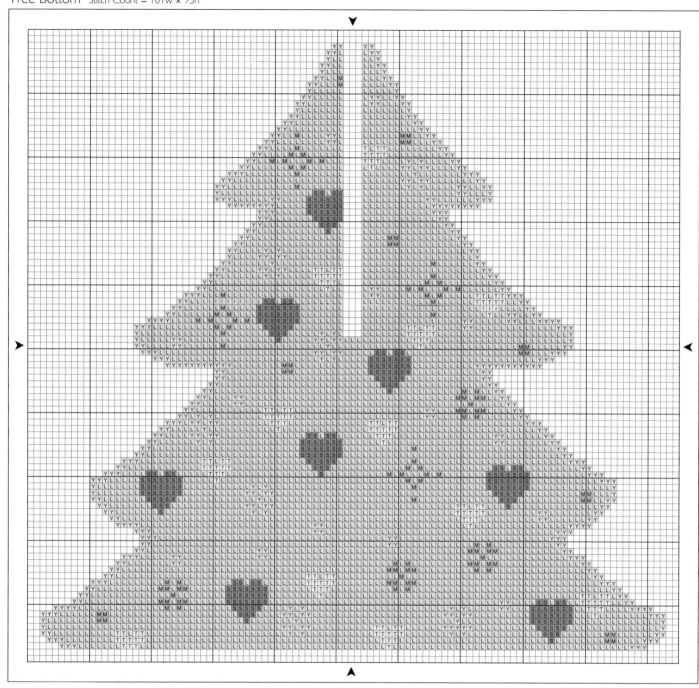

## 3-D Trees

### Fabric
**(per finished tree)**

- Four 8¼" × 11" pieces of 14-ct. Clear Perforated Plastic

### Design Size

- Tree Top:
  14-ct. = 7¼" × 8"
- Tree Bottom:
  14-ct. = 7¼" × 6¾"

### General Instructions

Center the design and begin stitching. Work cross-stitches with two strands of cotton embroidery floss. Stitch each chart twice in each colorway, as each finished tree requires two Tree Top sections and two Tree Bottom sections. Trim to within one unstitched row.

### Finishing Instructions

With the wrong sides of two matching Tree Top pieces together, overcast around the tree with DMC 3756 to join. Repeat with two matching Tree Bottom pieces. Slot the Tree Top into the Tree Bottom to complete the tree.

Slotted Tree 1:
CROSS-STITCH

| ANCHOR | | DMC | COLOR |
|---|---|---|---|
| 281 | L | 580 | Dark Moss Green |
| 874 | T | 834 | Very Light Golden Olive |
| 897 | S | 902 | Very Dark Garnet |
| 1023 | M | 3712 | Medium Salmon |
| 1037 | Y | 3756 | Ultra Very Light Baby Blue |

Slotted Tree 2:
CROSS-STITCH

| ANCHOR | | DMC | COLOR |
|---|---|---|---|
| 280 | T | 733 | Medium Olive Green |
| 045 | M | 814 | Dark Garnet |
| 842 | L | 3013 | Light Khaki Green |
| 059 | S | 3350 | Ultra Dark Dusty Rose |
| 1037 | Y | 3756 | Ultra Very Light Baby Blue |

Slotted Tree 3:
CROSS-STITCH

| ANCHOR | | DMC | COLOR |
|---|---|---|---|
| 010 | T | 351 | Coral |
| 280 | L | 733 | Medium Olive Green |
| 1005 | S | 816 | Garnet |
| 681 | M | 3051 | Dark Green Gray |
| 1037 | Y | 3756 | Ultra Very Light Baby Blue |

## Victorian Christmas

### Fabric
- One 16" × 20" piece of 28-ct. Doubloon Hand-Dyed Cashel® Linen (stitched over two threads)

### Design Size
- 28-ct. = 7½" × 11½"

### Embellishments
- 1 package of Victorian Gold #02011 glass seed beads by Mill Hill®

### Instructions
Center the design and begin stitching over two fabric threads. Work cross-stitches and quarter stitches with two strands of cotton embroidery floss or DMC Light Effects floss. Work backstitches with one strand of cotton embroidery floss or DMC Light Effects floss. Attach beads with one strand of coordinating floss. Lay the needlework facedown on a terry cloth towel (to protect beads) and use a pressing cloth to carefully iron the needlework from the back before framing as desired.

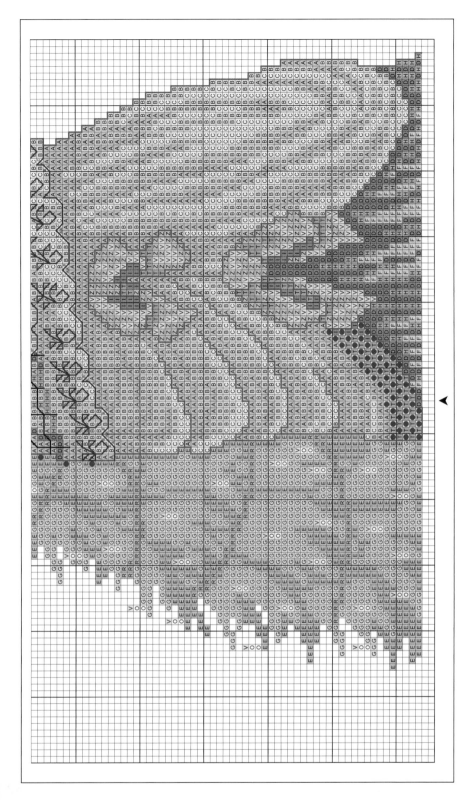

# Olive & Merlot

## CROSS-STITCH

| ANCHOR | | DMC | COLOR |
|---|---|---|---|
| 218 | E | 319 | Very Dark Pistachio Green |
| 013 | H | 349 | Dark Coral |
| 010 | F | 351 | Coral |
| 006 | K | 353 | Peach |
| 217 | G | 367 | Dark Pistachio Green |
| 358 | S | 433 | Medium Brown |
| 1046 | P | 435 | Very Light Brown |
| 362 | M | 437 | Light Tan |
| 266 | B | 470 | Light Avocado Green |
| 265 | C | 471 | Very Light Avocado Green |
| 305 | V | 728 | Topaz |
| 387 | Y | 739 | Ultra Very Light Tan |
| 1012 | L | 754 | Light Peach |
| 309 | I | 781 | Very Dark Topaz |
| 308 | T | 782 | Dark Topaz |
| 307 | Z | 783 | Medium Topaz |
| 013 | D | 817 | Very Dark Coral Red |
| 268 | A | 937 | Medium Avocado Green |
| 381 | U | 938 | Ultra Dark Coffee Brown |
| 1011 | J | 948 | Very Light Peach |
| 397 | N | 3024 | Very Light Brown Gray |
| 002 | O | 3865 | Winter White |
| DMC LIGHT EFFECTS | | COLOR | |
| E677 | R | White Gold | |

## BACKSTITCH

| ANCHOR | | DMC | COLOR |
|---|---|---|---|
| 013 | —— | 817 | Very Dark Coral Red |
| 381 | —— | 938 | Ultra Dark Coffee Brown |
| DMC LIGHT EFFECTS | | COLOR | |
| E677 | —— | White Gold | |

## BEAD

| MILL HILL GLASS SEED | | COLOR |
|---|---|---|
| 02011 | ● | Victorian Gold |

## Project Tip

### Stitching with Seed Beads

Seed beads require very fine needles that will slide through the holes. Two readily available options are a #8 quilting needle, which is short with a tiny eye, and a long beading needle, which has a longer eye.

**Sleigh** Stitch Count = 53w × 47h

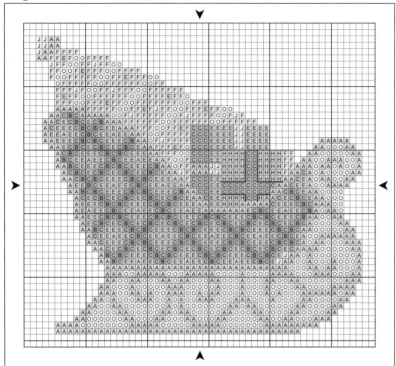

**Stocking** Stitch Count = 38w × 58h

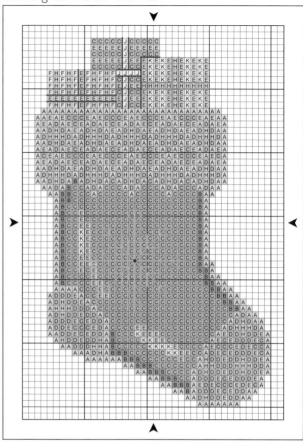

**Mittens** Stitch Count = 53w × 43h

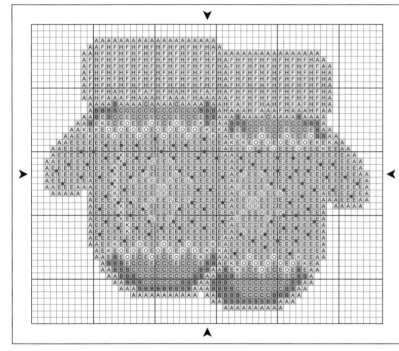

## Tiny Treasures

### Fabric (each design)
- One 6" × 7" piece of 14-ct. Clear Perforated Plastic

### Design Size
- Sleigh: 14-ct. = 3¾" × 3⅜"
- Stocking: 14-ct. = 2¾" × 4⅛"
- Mittens: 14-ct. = 3¾" × 3"
- Soldier: 14-ct. = 2¼" × 4¾"
- Ornament: 14-ct. = 3¼" × 3¾"
- Cardinal: 14-ct. = 3¾" × 3⅝"
- Poinsettia: 14-ct. = 3¼" × 3½"
- Tree: 14-ct. = 3¼" × 3⅞"
- Bell: 14-ct. = 3" × 3⅞"

Olive & Merlot

**Soldier** Stitch Count = 32w × 66h

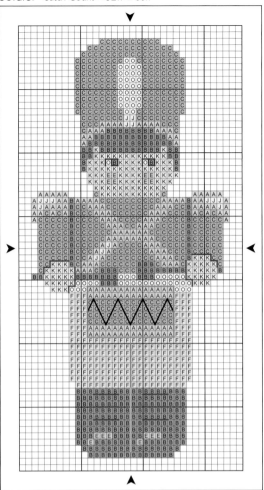

**Ornament** Stitch Count = 45w × 53h

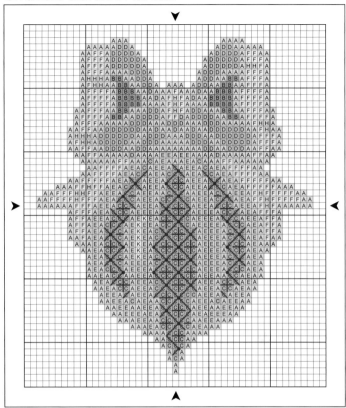

**Cardinal** Stitch Count = 53w × 51h

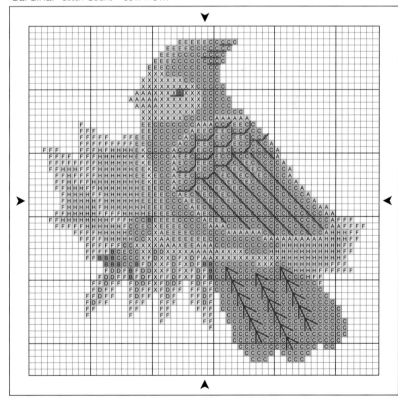

- **Finishing Materials (each design)**
- 4" × 5" piece of white felt
- 5" length of coordinating ribbon
- Clear quick-dry craft glue

## Instructions

Center the design and begin stitching. Work cross-stitches with two strands of cotton embroidery floss. Work backstitches, straight stitches, and French knots with 1 strand of cotton embroidery floss. Trim the needlework to within one unstitched row. Affix a ribbon to the top back as a hanger. Trim the felt to the same size and shape as the design and affix to the back of the ornament.

### CROSS-STITCH

| ANCHOR | | DMC | COLOR |
|---|---|---|---|
| 001 | O | B5200 | Snow White |
| 1026 | K | 225 | Ultra Very Light Shell Pink |
| 403 | X | 310 | Black |
| 897 | B | 902 | Very Dark Garnet |
| 268 | D | 3345 | Dark Hunter Green |
| 267 | F | 3346 | Hunter Green |
| 266 | H | 3347 | Medium Yellow Green |
| 1018 | E | 3726 | Dark Antique Mauve |
| 1019 | C | 3802 | Ultra Very Dark Antique Mauve |
| 306 | A | 3820 | Dark Straw |
| 295 | J | 3822 | Light Straw |

### FRENCH KNOT

| ANCHOR | | DMC | COLOR |
|---|---|---|---|
| 001 | ● | B5200 | Snow White |
| 295 | ● | 3822 | Light Straw |

### BACKSTITCH

| ANCHOR | | DMC | COLOR |
|---|---|---|---|
| 001 | —— | B5200 | Snow White |

### BACKSTITCH

| ANCHOR | | DMC | COLOR |
|---|---|---|---|
| 897 | —— | 902 | Very Dark Garnet |
| 268 | —— | 3345 | Dark Hunter Green |
| 306 | —— | 3820 | Dark Straw |

### STRAIGHT STITCH

| ANCHOR | | DMC | COLOR |
|---|---|---|---|
| 001 | —— | B5200 | Snow White |

*Note:* Not all colors are used in each design.

**Poinsettia** Stitch Count = 46w × 49h

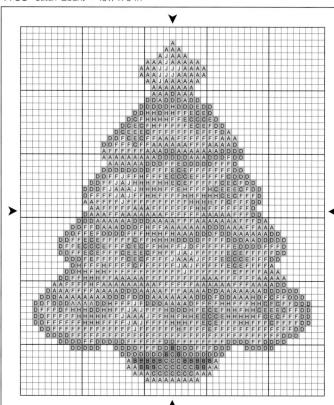

**Tree** Stitch Count = 45w × 54h

# Olive & Merlot

**Bell** Stitch Count = 42w × 54h

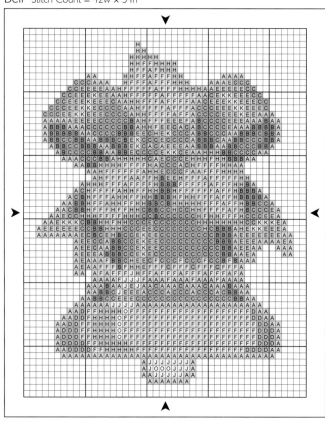

<table>
<tr><td colspan="4">CROSS-STITCH</td></tr>
</table>

| ANCHOR | | DMC | COLOR |
|---|---|---|---|
| 001 | O | B5200 | Snow White |
| 1026 | K | 225 | Ultra Very Light Shell Pink |
| 897 | B | 902 | Very Dark Garnet |
| 268 | D | 3345 | Dark Hunter Green |
| 267 | F | 3346 | Hunter Green |
| 266 | H | 3347 | Medium Yellow Green |

**CROSS-STITCH**

| ANCHOR | | DMC | COLOR |
|---|---|---|---|
| 1018 | E | 3726 | Dark Antique Mauve |
| 1019 | C | 3802 | Ultra Very Dark Antique Mauve |
| 306 | A | 3820 | Dark Straw |
| 295 | J | 3822 | Light Straw |

*Note:* Not all colors are used in each design.

## Project Tip

**Stitching on Perforated Plastic**

Perforated plastic does not stretch to accommodate multiple strands of floss in each hole as aida or linen do. When stitching on perforated plastic, choose a sharp, pointed needle (not a blunt-tip one), as it will glide more easily through the holes that have already been stitched through. If desired, you can overcast the edge of the ornament for a more finished look. With one undivided strand of embroidery floss, anchor the floss on the wrong side of the needlework and work your needle from the outside in.

## Noel Hoop

### Fabric

• One 14" × 14" piece of 28-ct. Antique White Cashel® Linen (stitched over two threads)

### Design Size

• 28-ct. = 5½" × 5⅝"

### Embellishments

• 1 package each of Old Gold #00557 glass seed beads by Mill Hill®

### Finishing Materials

• 7" × 9¼" white fabric
• Matching sewing thread
• Magnetic scroll hanger frame

### General Instructions

Center the design and begin stitching over two fabric threads. Work cross-stitches with two strands of cotton embroidery floss or DMC® Color Variations. To maximize color changes when stitching with variegated floss, complete each cross-stitch before moving on to the next one. Work backstitches, straight stitches, and French knots with one strand of cotton embroidery floss or Kreinik (very fine) #4 braid. Attach beads with one strand of coordinating floss. Lay the needlework face down on a terry cloth towel (to protect beads) and use a pressing cloth to carefully iron the needlework from the back before finishing.

### Finishing Instructions

Use a ¼" seam allowance for all sewing unless otherwise specified.

Noel Hoop   Stitch Count = 78w × 79h

Center and trim the needlework to 7" × 9¼". With right sides together, sew to the white fabric back along the left and right edges. Turn and press. Following the manufacturer's instructions, insert into a magnetic scroll hanger frame.

### CROSS-STITCH

| ANCHOR | | DMC | COLOR |
|---|---|---|---|
| 310 | C | 434 | Light Brown |
| 1045 | D | 436 | Tan |
| 361 | E | 738 | Very Light Tan |
| 360 | B | 898 | Very Dark Coffee Brown |
| 1028 | J | 3685 | Very Dark Mauve |
| 068 | L | 3687 | Medium Mauve |
| 972 | K | 3803 | Dark Mauve |

| DMC COLOR VARIATIONS | | COLOR |
|---|---|---|
| 4045 | P | Evergreen Forest |
| 4210 | M | Radiant Ruby |

### FRENCH KNOT

| ANCHOR | DMC | COLOR |
|---|---|---|
| 382 | ● 3371 | Black Brown |

### BACKSTITCH

| ANCHOR | DMC | COLOR |
|---|---|---|
| 382 | ——3371 | Black Brown |

| KREINIK BRAID #4 | COLOR |
|---|---|
| 002 | —— Gold |

### STRAIGHT STITCH

| ANCHOR | DMC | COLOR |
|---|---|---|
| 246 | —— 986 | Very Dark Forest Green |
| 244 | —— 987 | Dark Forest Green |
| 242 | —— 989 | Forest Green |

### SMYRNA CROSS

| KREINIK BRAID #4 | COLOR |
|---|---|
| 002 | Gold |

### DIAMOND EYELET

| KREINIK BRAID #4 | COLOR |
|---|---|
| 002 | Gold |

### BEAD

| MILL HILL GLASS SEED | COLOR |
|---|---|
| 00557 | ● Old Gold |

**Smyrna Cross**

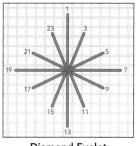

**Diamond Eyelet**

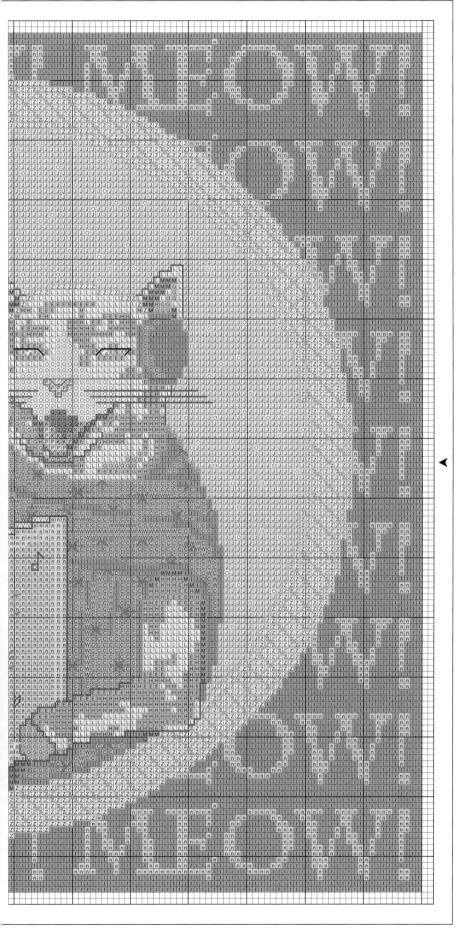

## Caroling Kitties

### Fabric
- One 20" × 17" piece of 32-ct. White Belfast® Linen (stitched over two threads)

### Design Size
- 32-ct. = 11¾" × 9"

### Instructions
Center the design and begin stitching over two fabric threads. Work cross-stitches and quarter stitches with two strands of cotton embroidery floss or DMC® Light Effects floss. Work backstitches with one strand of cotton embroidery floss or DMC Light Effects floss. Use a pressing cloth to carefully iron the needlework from the back before framing as desired.

### CROSS-STITCH

| ANCHOR | | DMC | COLOR |
|---|---|---|---|
| 387 | V | Ecru | Ecru |
| 001 | O | B5200 | Snow White |
| 403 | X | 310 | Black |
| 400 | L | 317 | Pewter Gray |
| 399 | E | 318 | Light Steel Gray |
| 401 | H | 413 | Dark Pewter Gray |
| 232 | N | 452 | Medium Shell Gray |
| 231 | R | 453 | Light Shell Gray |
| 1038 | J | 519 | Sky Blue |
| 055 | P | 604 | Light Cranberry |
| 361 | F | 738 | Very Light Tan |
| 234 | G | 762 | Very Light Pearl Gray |
| 1044 | n | 895 | Very Dark Hunter Green |
| 1003 | T | 921 | Copper |
| 1002 | Y | 977 | Light Golden Brown |
| 266 | S | 3347 | Medium Yellow Green |
| 264 | D | 3348 | Light Yellow Green |
| 086 | W | 3608 | Very Light Plum |
| 068 | C | 3687 | Medium Mauve |
| 1020 | U | 3713 | Very Light Salmon |
| 076 | K | 3731 | Very Dark Dusty Rose |
| 1007 | h | 3772 | Very Dark Desert Sand |
| 236 | M | 3799 | Very Dark Pewter Gray |
| 1019 | B | 3802 | Ultra Very Dark Antique Mauve |
| 972 | I | 3803 | Dark Mauve |
| 936 | A | 3857 | Dark Rosewood |
| 1007 | Q | 3858 | Medium Rosewood |

| DMC LIGHT EFFECTS | | COLOR |
|---|---|---|
| E3821 | Z | Light Gold |

### BACKSTITCH

| ANCHOR | DMC | COLOR |
|---|---|---|
| 001 | B5200 | Snow White |
| 403 | 310 | Black |
| 234 | 762 | Very Light Pearl Gray |
| 308 | 782 | Dark Topaz |
| 1044 | 895 | Very Dark Hunter Green |
| 1003 | 921 | Copper |
| 264 | 3348 | Light Yellow Green |
| 076 | 3731 | Very Dark Dusty Rose |
| 1007 | 3772 | Very Dark Desert Sand |
| 236 | 3799 | Very Dark Pewter Gray |
| 1019 | 3802 | Ultra Very Dark Antique Mauve |
| 936 | 3857 | Dark Rosewood |

### BACKSTITCH

| DMC LIGHT EFFECTS | COLOR |
|---|---|
| 3821 | Light Gold |

# Pretty
## Pastels

*Daylight dawns on a glittering winter wonderland filled with whimsical hand-stitched displays of holiday magic.*

The soft, pastel hues and subtle pops of shimmer bring to mind the joy of a bright, snowy morning just waiting to be explored. And what a glorious collection of surprises you'll find! Journey into the winter landscape with Lee Fisher's radiant Queen of the North or spend some time with fanciful nutcrackers, sweet Arctic animals, or a trio of ships sailing in to harbor. You'll be inspired all season long by their bright, delicate charm.

**Project instructions begin on page 75.**

*Characters of Tchaikovsky's The Nutcracker*
are given a sugarplum makeover in these adorable standing figures
designed by Frony Ritter. The addition of blending filament and
eye-catching seed beads make these pieces show-ready!

**Project instructions begin on page 72.**

# Pretty Pastels

*Listen as this demure angel
sweetly sings her Christmas
greetings for all to hear.*
Emma Congdon's signature use of
color and pattern make this little
cherub a delightful project to stitch
and a unique holiday decoration.

**Project instructions begin on page 74.**

*Folk-art forest dwellers designed by Diane Machin reside in a charming rose-colored landscape* that will delight your Christmas card recipients. These quick-to-stitch designs will become a go-to for holiday greetings!

**Project instructions begin on page 78.**

*Discover all of the charming details in this expansive holiday greeting* designed by Durene Jones. From cute characters to folksy hearts and snowflakes, you'll want to display this ombré masterpiece where everyone can see.

**Project instructions begin on page 84.**

Pretty Pastels

*A classic Christmas carol gets a colorful update*
with this unique design by Erik Shipley. Sing along as you work
with entrancing shades of variegated floss on an irresistible blue,
hand-dyed fabric.

**Project instructions begin on page 80.**

# Pretty Pastels

*This effortless arrangement
of pretty poinsettias and
snowflakes* designed by Kathleen
Berlew makes for a splendid winter
garden. Display your handiwork all
winter as a cozy pillow with amazing
pastel buffalo check.

**Project instructions begin on page 82**

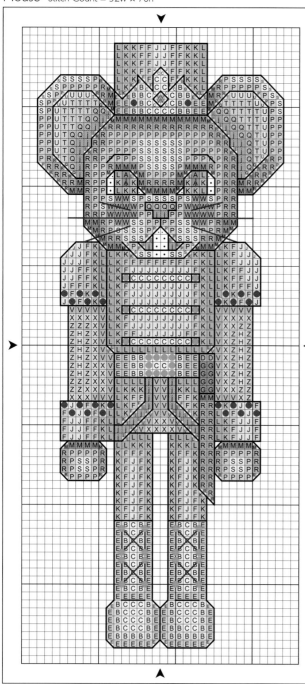

## Pretty Pastels

### Nutcracker Trio

#### Fabric (each design)
- One 9" × 12" piece of 14-ct. White Aida

#### Design Size
- Mouse: 14-ct. = 2¼" × 5½"
- Fairy: 14-ct. = 3⅛" × 6"
- Man: 14-ct. = 2" × 6"

#### Embellishments
- 1 package each of Iris #00252, Light Green #00525, and Bahama Blue #02097 glass seed beads by Mill Hill®

#### Finishing Materials
- ¼ yard of blue fabric
- Fiberfill
- 3 yards of white pom-pom trim
- Matching sewing thread

#### General Instructions
Center the design and begin stitching. Work cross-stitches and quarter stitches with two strands of cotton embroidery floss. Work blended stitches with two strands of cotton embroidery floss and one strand of Kreinik Blending Filament. Work backstitches and straight stitches with one strand of cotton embroidery floss. Attach beads with one strand of coordinating floss.
 Lay the needlework facedown on a terry cloth towel (to protect beads) and use a pressing cloth to carefully iron the needlework from the back before finishing.

#### Finishing Instructions
Use a ¼" seam allowance for all sewing unless otherwise specified. Trim the needlewor to within 1¼" of the stitching on the left, right, and top edges and to within 1¾" of the stitching on the bottom edge. Referring to the photo, trim into a rounded shape as desir

 Cut a piece of blue fabric the same size and shape as the needlework. With right sides together, sew the needlework front and backing fabric together, leaving the bottom open. Press the seam open, turn, and press the fabric around the opening ¼" to the inside. Stuff with fiberfill. Cut two pieces of pom-pom trim 2 longer than the length of the entire rounded seam. Hand-stitch the trim in place to cove the seam, tucking the excess trim into the fiberfill.

 Measure the rounded opening on the bottom and cut a piece of blue fabric that ½" wider and ½" taller. Press t excess fabric ¼" to the wrong side around the entire edge. With right side out, hand-stitc in place to cover the opening at the bottom of the figure.

### CROSS-STITCH

| ANCHOR | | DMC | COLOR |
|---|---|---|---|
| 002 | · | White | White |
| 1096 | S | 002 | Tin |
| 110 | Y | 208 | Very Dark Lavender |
| 109 | e | 209 | Dark Lavender |
| 108 | m | 210 | Medium Lavender |
| 342 | r | 211 | Light Lavender |
| 399 | R | 318 | Light Steel Gray |
| 235 | M | 414 | Dark Steel Gray |
| 398 | P | 415 | Pearl Gray |

### CROSS-STITCH

| ANCHOR | | DMC | COLOR |
|---|---|---|---|
| 358 | G | 433 | Medium Brown |
| 1046 | D | 435 | Very Light Brown |
| 055 | j | 604 | Light Cranberry |
| 050 | Q | 605 | Very Light Cranberry |
| 303 | E | 742 | Light Tangerine |
| 302 | B | 743 | Medium Yellow |
| 301 | C | 744 | Pale Yellow |
| 1012 | b | 754 | Light Peach |
| 882 | N | 758 | Very Light Terra Cotta |

### CROSS-STITCH

| ANCHOR | | DMC | COLOR |
|---|---|---|---|
| 1022 | W | 760 | Salmon |
| 128 | H | 775 | Very Light Baby Blue |
| 161 | V | 813 | Light Blue |
| 205 | L | 911 | Medium Emerald Green |
| 204 | K | 913 | Medium Nile Green |
| 203 | F | 954 | Nile Green |
| 206 | J | 955 | Light Nile Green |
| 905 | A | 3021 | Very Dark Brown Gray |
| 129 | X | 3325 | Light Baby Blue |

**Fairy** Stitch Count = 43w × 84h

**Man** Stitch Count = 27w × 84h

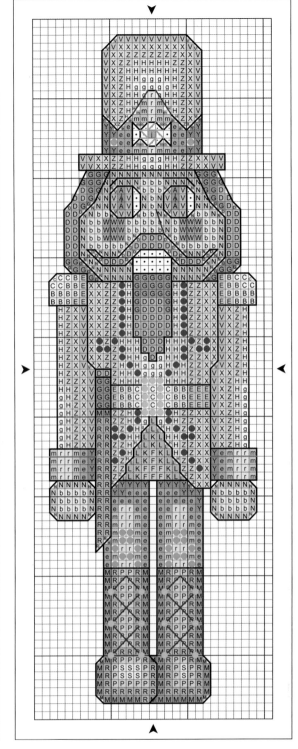

### CROSS-STITCH

| ANCHOR | | DMC | COLOR |
|---|---|---|---|
| 049 | T | 3689 | Light Mauve |
| 1037 | g | 3756 | Ultra Very Light Baby Blue |
| 9159 | Z | 3841 | Pale Baby Blue |

### BACKSTITCH

| ANCHOR | | DMC | COLOR |
|---|---|---|---|
| 1096 | —— | 002 | Tin |
| 110 | —— | 208 | Very Dark Lavender |
| 055 | —— | 604 | Light Cranberry |
| 205 | —— | 911 | Medium Emerald Green |
| 905 | —— | 3021 | Very Dark Brown Gray |

### STRAIGHT STITCH

| ANCHOR | | DMC | COLOR |
|---|---|---|---|
| 905 | —— | 3021 | Very Dark Brown Gray |

### BEAD

| MILL HILL GLASS SEED | | COLOR |
|---|---|---|
| 00252 | ● | Iris |
| 00525 | ● | Light Green |
| 02097 | ● | Bahama Blue |

*Note:* Not all colors are used in each design.

## Merry Christmas Angel

### Fabric
- One 15" × 16" piece of 25-ct. Angel Blush Lugana (stitched over two threads)

### Design Size
- 25-ct. = 6⅜" × 8"

### Finishing Materials
- ¼ yard of pink fabric
- 8" × 11" piece of lightweight fusible interfacing
- Matching sewing thread

### General Instructions
Center the design and begin stitching over two fabric threads. Work cross stitches with two strands of cotton embroidery floss or DMC® Light Effects floss. Use a pressing cloth to carefully iron the needlework from the back before finishing.

### Finishing Instructions
Use a ¼" seam allowance for all sewing unless specified. Center the interfacing on the wrong side of the needlework and, following the manufacturer's instructions, fuse into place. Trim to within 1¾" of the stitching on the top and ¾" of the stitching on the sides and bottom.

Cut a piece of pink fabric the same size as the front. With right sides together, sew the front to the back, leaving an opening on the top. Turn right side out and press. Whipstitch the opening closed. Fold the top 1" to the back and hand-stitch in place. Hang as desired.

### CROSS-STITCH

| ANCHOR | | DMC | COLOR |
|---|---|---|---|
| 342 | J | 211 | Light Lavender |
| 895 | Y | 223 | Light Shell Pink |
| 119 | T | 333 | Very Dark Blue Violet |
| 118 | S | 340 | Medium Blue Violet |
| 009 | A | 352 | Light Coral |
| 943 | M | 422 | Light Hazelnut Brown |
| 168 | W | 597 | Turquoise |
| 167 | D | 598 | Light Turquoise |
| 158 | P | 747 | Very Light Sky Blue |
| 128 | F | 775 | Very Light Baby Blue |
| 023 | L | 818 | Baby Pink |

### CROSS-STITCH

| ANCHOR | | DMC | COLOR |
|---|---|---|---|
| 050 | K | 957 | Pale Geranium |
| 073 | V | 963 | Ultra Very Light Dusty Rose |
| 185 | C | 964 | Light Sea Green |
| 264 | N | 3348 | Light Yellow Green |
| 1030 | H | 3746 | Dark Blue Violet |
| 1032 | R | 3752 | Very Light Antique Blue |
| 140 | G | 3755 | Baby Blue |

| DMC LIGHT EFFECTS | | | COLOR |
|---|---|---|---|
| | E5200 | U | Snow White |
| | E677 | B | White Gold |

## Queen of the North

### Fabric
- One 19" × 19" piece of 28-ct. Sprite Hand-Dyed Cashel (stitched over two threads)

### Design Size
- 28-ct. = 10⅝" × 10½"

### Embellishments
- 1 package of Ice #62010 frosted glass seed beads by Mill Hill®

### Instructions
Center the design and begin stitching over two fabric threads. Work cross-stitches, quarter stitches, and backstitches with two strands of cotton embroidery floss. Attach beads with one strand of coordinating floss. Lay the needlework facedown on a terry cloth towel (to protect beads) and use a pressing cloth to carefully iron the needlework from the back before framing as desired.

| A | B |
|---|---|
| C | D |

# Pretty Pastels

Queen of the North
Stitch Count = 149w × 147h

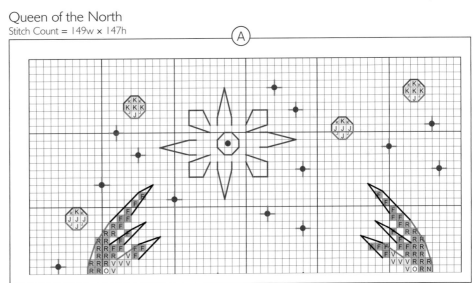

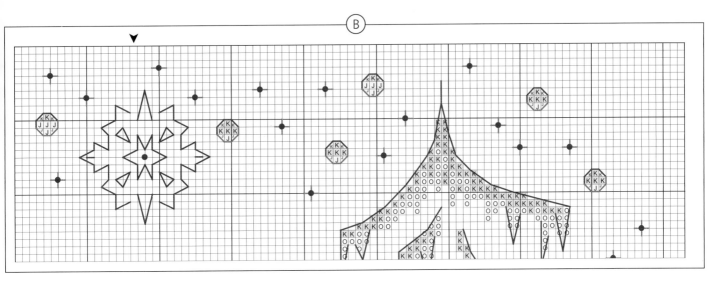

## CROSS-STITCH

| ANCHOR | | DMC | COLOR |
|---|---|---|---|
| 001 | O | B5200 | Snow White |
| 400 | F | 317 | Pewter Gray |
| 399 | R | 318 | Light Steel Gray |
| 398 | N | 415 | Pearl Gray |
| 168 | D | 597 | Turquoise |
| 158 | K | 747 | Very Light Sky Blue |
| 1012 | M | 754 | Light Peach |
| 234 | V | 762 | Very Light Pearl Gray |
| 1011 | G | 948 | Very Light Peach |
| 778 | L | 3774 | Very Light Desert Sand |
| 779 | H | 3809 | Very Dark Turquoise |
| 168 | E | 3810 | Dark Turquoise |
| 928 | J | 3811 | Very Light Turquoise |

## BACKSTITCH

| ANCHOR | | DMC | COLOR |
|---|---|---|---|
| 001 | —— | B5200 | Snow White |
| 400 | —— | 317 | Pewter Gray |
| 399 | —— | 318 | Light Steel Gray |
| 158 | —— | 747 | Very Light Sky Blue |
| 1012 | —— | 754 | Light Peach |
| 779 | —— | 3809 | Very Dark Turquoise |

## BEAD

| MILL HILL GLASS SEED | | COLOR |
|---|---|---|
| 62010 | ● | Frosted Ice |

## Project Tip

**Determining the Center of the Fabric**

Unless otherwise indicated, always begin stitching the center of your design in the center of the fabric. To determine the exact center of the fabric, fold the fabric in quarters. Draw a strand of floss through the fabric at this point to mark the center. For some projects, it is helpful to baste along the two fold lines. Always use light-colored floss for basting so the floss does not leave any marks when it is removed. The point where the basting lines cross is the center of the fabric. When your stitching is complete, remove all basting stitches.

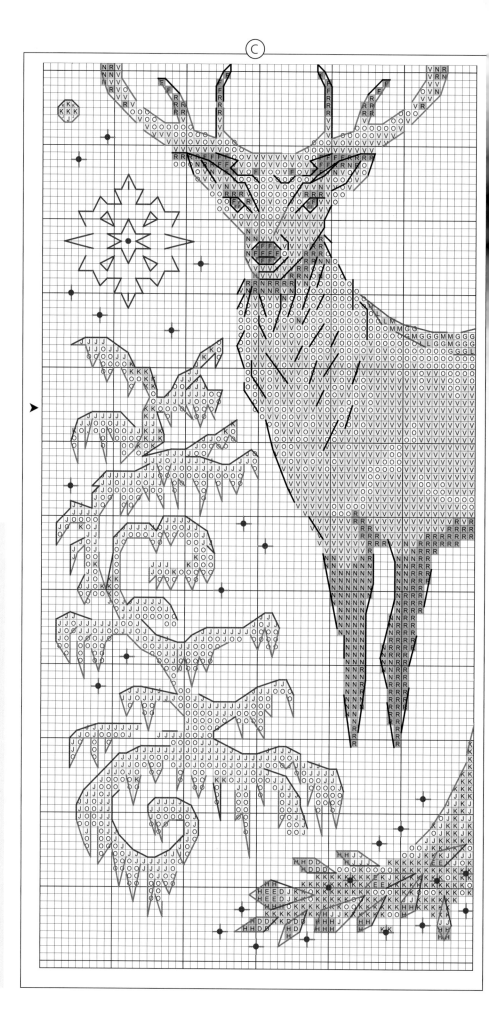

**Bear** Stitch Count = 57w × 54h

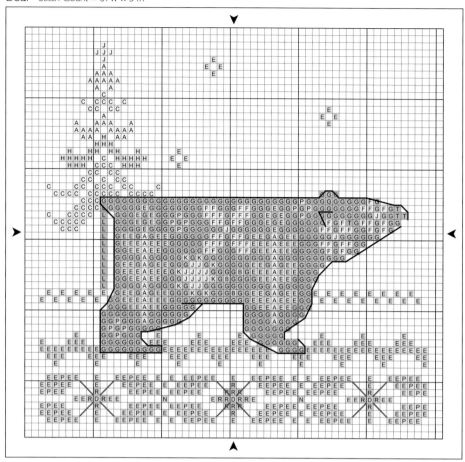

**Squirrel** Stitch Count = 56w × 55h

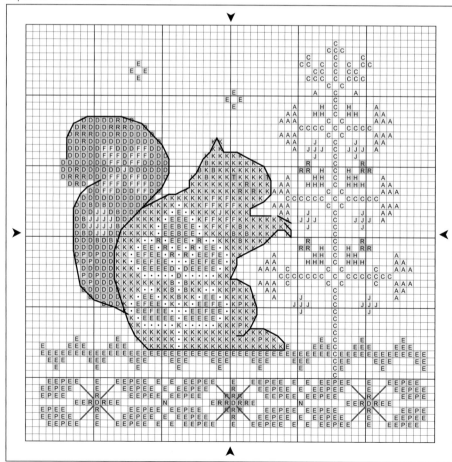

## Woodland Animal Minis

**Fabric (each design)**
- One 7" × 7" piece of 14-ct. Bo Peep Pink Aida

**Design Size (each design)**
- Fox, Bear, & Rabbit: 14-ct. = 4" × 3⅞"
- Squirrel: 14-ct. = 4" × 4"

**Finishing Materials**
- Four 11" × 5½" pieces of white cardstock
- Pencil
- Craft knife
- Double-sided tape
- Coordinating embroidery floss
- Metallic cording

### General Instructions

Center the design and begin stitching. Work cross-stitches and quarter stitches with two strands of cotton embroidery floss. Work backstitches with one strand of cotton embroidery floss. Use a pressing cloth to carefully iron the needlework from the back before finishing.

### Finishing Instructions

Center and trim the needlework to 5¼" × 5¼". Fold the cardstock in half to make a 5½" × 5½" side-opening card. Mark a 4½" × 4½" square on the front of the card. Using a craft knife, cut out the square, rounding the corners if desired. Center the needlework in the opening and adhere to the four borders with double-sided tape.

Cut two 18" pieces of cotton floss or metallic cording. Hold the pieces together, wrap around the left edge near the fold, and tie a bow.

### CROSS-STITCH

| ANCHOR | | DMC | COLOR | |
|--------|---|-------|-------|---|
| 002 | • | White | White | |
| 342 | S | 211 | Light Lavender | |
| 214 | N | 368 | Light Pistachio Green | |
| 1043 | A | 369 | Very Light Pistachio Green | |
| 050 | E | 605 | Very Light Cranberry | |
| 160 | D | 827 | Very Light Blue | |
| 1010 | J | 951 | Light Tawny | |
| 206 | P | 955 | Light Nile Green | |
| 185 | H | 964 | Light Sea Green | |
| 883 | L | 3064 | Desert Sand | |

# Pretty
## Pastels

## Project Tip

### Create Woodland Ornaments

These whimsical designs would also make cute ornaments. Center and trim the needlework to within 1" of the stitching on all sides. Center and affix to the adhesive side of a 4" x 4" piece of self-adhesive mounting board. Wrap the fabric to the back and glue. Use craft glue to affix a piece of ribbon to the back as a hanger and line the back with a piece of coordinating felt.

**Rabbit** Stitch Count = 57w × 54h

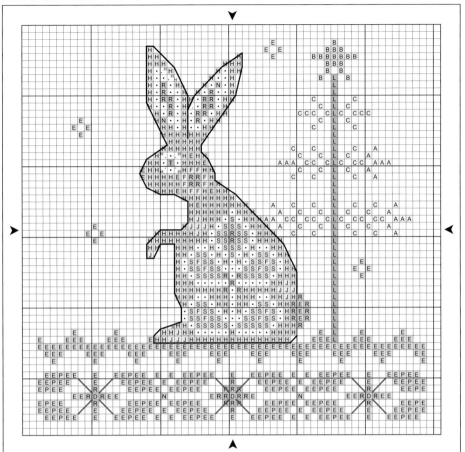

**Fox** Stitch Count = 57w × 54h

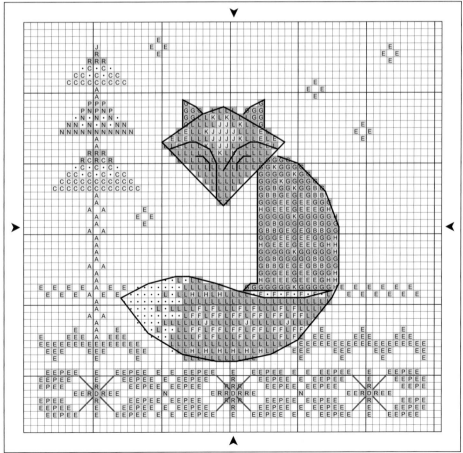

## CROSS-STITCH

| ANCHOR | | DMC | COLOR |
|---|---|---|---|
| 1037 | F | 3756 | Ultra Very Light Baby Blue |
| 236 | T | 3799 | Very Dark Pewter Gray |
| 278 | C | 3819 | Light Moss Green |
| 187 | R | 3851 | Bright Green |
| 311 | B | 3855 | Light Autumn Gold |

## BACKSTITCH

| ANCHOR | | DMC | COLOR |
|---|---|---|---|
| 050 | —— | 605 | Very Light Cranberry |
| 236 | —— | 3799 | Very Dark Pewter Gray |

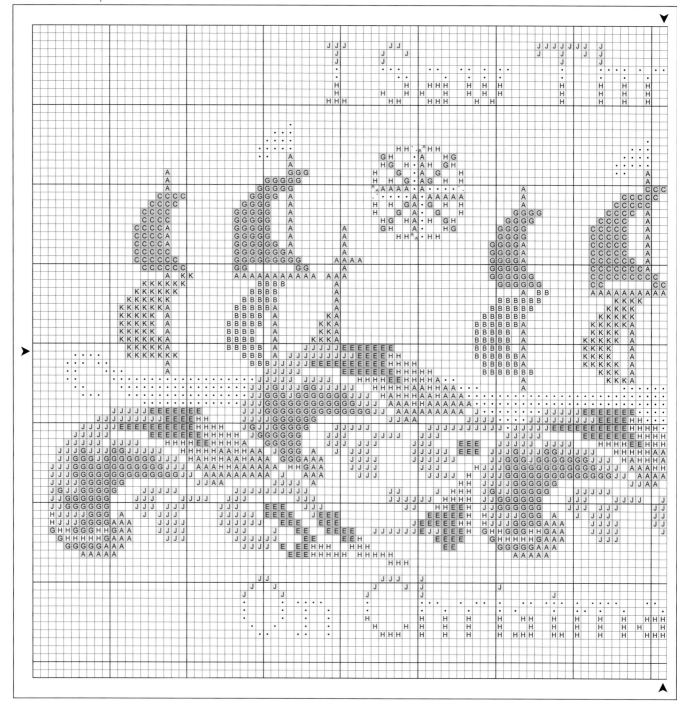

## I Saw Three Ships

**Fabric**
- One 18" × 13" piece of 18-ct. Beachy Keen Hand-Dyed Aida

**Design Size**
- 18-ct. = 8⅞" × 4⅜"

**Finishing Materials**
- Two 10" × 5½" pieces of mat board
- 13" × 8" piece of teal print fabric
- 13" × 8" piece of cotton batting
- 1½ yards of ¼" rickrack

- Basting spray
- Clear quick-dry craft glue

**General Instructions**
Center the design and begin stitching. Work cross-stitches and half-stitches with two strands of cotton embroidery floss. Use a pressing cloth to carefully iron the needlework from the back before finishing.

**Finishing Instructions**
Center and trim the needlework to within 2" of the stitching on all sides. Cut a piece of teal print fabric the same size as the needlework. Trim the corners of each piece of mat board so they are slightly rounded. Lightly spray one of the mat board pieces with basting spray and place glue-side down on the cotton batting. Trim batting to the edges of the board. Mount the needlework on the piece of batting-covered board. Use craft glue to adhere the edges of the fabric to the back.

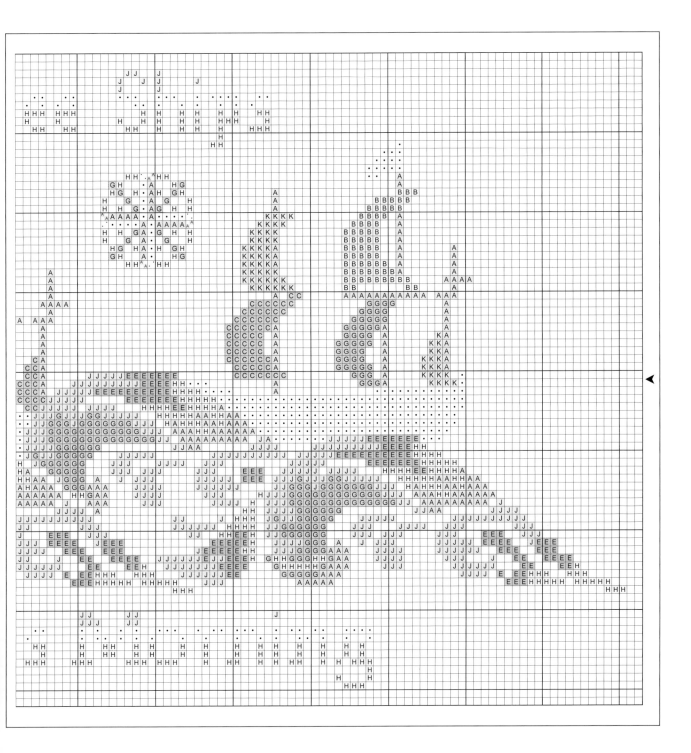

Use basting spray to mount the teal print fabric to the remaining piece of trimmed mat board. Glue the edges to the back. Cut a 12" piece of rickrack. Bring the edges together and tie a knot 4" from the center of the loop. Glue the ends below the knot at the center top of the wrong side for a hanger.

With wrong sides together, glue the front and back pieces together. Glue rickrack around the edge to cover the seam.

## Pretty Pastels

### CROSS-STITCH

| ANCHOR | | DMC | COLOR |
|---|---|---|---|
| 002 | • | White | White |
| 108 | A | 210 | Medium Lavender |
| 1038 | E | 519 | Sky Blue |
| 055 | G | 604 | Light Cranberry |
| 293 | B | 727 | Very Light Topaz |
| 144 | H | 800 | Pale Delft Blue |
| 206 | J | 955 | Light Nile Green |
| 008 | C | 3824 | Light Apricot |
| 311 | K | 3855 | Light Autumn Gold |

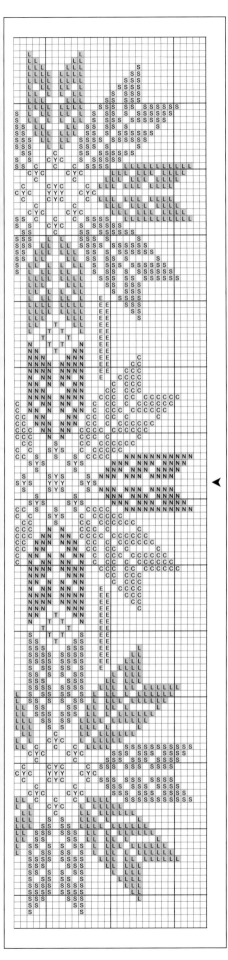

## Poinsettias & Snowflakes

### Fabric

• One 18" × 18" piece of 25-ct. White Lugana (stitched over two threads)

### Design Size

• 25-ct. = 10½" × 10½"

### Finishing Materials

• 1 yard of pastel plaid fabric
• ¼ yard of mint fabric
• 11" × 11" piece of lightweight fusible interfacing
• Matching sewing thread
• Masking tape

### General Instructions

Center the design and begin stitching over two fabric threads. Work cross-stitches with two strands of cotton embroidery floss. Use a pressing cloth to carefully iron the needlework from the back before finishing.

### Finishing Instructions

Use a ¼" seam allowance for all sewing unless otherwise specified. Center and trim the needlework to 11" × 11". Center the interfacing on the wrong side of the needlework and, following the manufacturer's directions, fuse into place. Cut two ½" × 11" pieces of mint fabric. With right sides together, sew to the top and bottom edges of the needlework. Cut two ½" × 11½" pieces of mint fabric. With right sides together, sew to the side edges of the needlework.

Cut four pastel print border strips, each 2¾" × 16". With right sides together, center and sew border strips on the right and left edges of the needlework. Excess length will extend beyond each edge. Press seams toward the strips. Sew the top and bottom border strips in the same manner.

Fold the top border strip under so it meets the edge of the side border and forms a 45-degree angle. Press in place. Pin the fold in place and check the angle to make sure the corner is flat and square. Carefully center a strip of masking tape over the mitered fold and secure. Turn the piece over.

On the wrong side of the fabric, draw a line slightly outside of the crease created when the fold was pressed. Beginning at the inside corner, backstitch and stitch on the line toward the outside point, being careful not to allow any stretching to occur. Backstitch at the end. Turn the piece over and remove the tape, checking to see that the corner lies flat. Trim the excess fabric to ¼" seam allowance and press. Repeat for other corners.

Cut two 16½ × 20" pieces of pastel print fabric. Fold and press each in half with wrong sides together to form two 16½" × 10" pieces. Overlap the pieces to create a pillow back that is the same size as the front. Baste the overlapping pieces in place. With right sides together, sew the pillow back and front together. Turn through the envelope opening and insert a pillow form.

# Pretty Pastels

CROSS-STITCH

| ANCHOR | | DMC | COLOR |
|---|---|---|---|
| 1030 | L | 155 | Medium Dark Blue Violet |
| 342 | S | 211 | Light Lavender |
| 167 | T | 598 | Light Turquoise |
| 295 | Y | 726 | Light Topaz |
| 128 | E | 775 | Very Light Baby Blue |
| 073 | C | 963 | Ultra Very Light Dusty Rose |
| 049 | N | 3689 | Very Light Mauve |

## Scrolling Merry Christmas

**Fabric**
- One 22" × 18" piece of 11-ct. White Aida

**Design Size**
- 11-ct. = 13½" × 9⅞"

**Instructions**

Center the design and begin stitching. Work cross-stitches and quarter stitches with two strands of cotton embroidery floss. Work backstitches with one strand of cotton embroidery floss. Use a pressing cloth to carefully iron the needlework from the back before framing as desired. *Note:* Metal hooks can be purchased and attached to the back of the framed piece to convert it into a scarf rack like the stitched model.

# Pretty Pastels

### CROSS-STITCH

| ANCHOR | | DMC | COLOR |
|---|---|---|---|
| 001 | O | B5200 | Snow White |
| 398 | D | 415 | Pearl Gray |
| 234 | E | 762 | Very Light Pearl Gray |
| 052 | M | 899 | Medium Rose |
| 1011 | N | 948 | Very Light Peach |
| 187 | B | 958 | Dark Sea Green |
| 073 | Q | 963 | Ultra Very Light Dusty Rose |
| 185 | C | 964 | Light Sea Green |
| 059 | L | 3350 | Ultra Dark Dusty Rose |
| 025 | P | 3716 | Very Light Dusty Rose |
| 928 | H | 3761 | Light Sky Blue |
| 167 | F | 3766 | Light Peacock Blue |
| 188 | A | 3814 | Aquamarine |
| 379 | S | 3863 | Medium Mocha Beige |
| 376 | T | 3864 | Light Mocha Beige |

### BACKSTITCH

| ANCHOR | DMC | COLOR |
|---|---|---|
| 042 | 309 | Dark Rose |
| 401 | 413 | Dark Pewter Gray |
| 188 | 3814 | Aquamarine |

# Gilded
## Greetings

*Set the scene for a holiday befitting royalty with this glitzy and glamourous treasury of cross-stitch delights.*

Rich shades of ginger, saffron, and paprika

paired with coordinating metallic tones elevate

your projects from basic to breathtaking.

Admire the scenes of the nativity with this

ethereal sampler designed by Barbara Sestok

to the tune of Silent Night, or light up the room

with shimmering candles, opulent ornaments,

or an awe-inspiring oversized biscornu. You will

be proud to offer such lavish handiwork as you

celebrate the season!

**Project instructions begin on page 93.**

*Turn Scandinavian styling on its head with a biscornu in shades of golden floss.* The amazing colorwork and symmetrical design of Jacob de Graaf results in something both traditional and modern.

**Project instructions begin on page 96.**

*Spice up your holiday gathering with this stitched recipe for mulled wine* designed by Alyssa Westhoek. The stylized instructions in fragrant colors will have guests clamoring for a glass of their own.

**Project instructions begin on page 98.**

# Gilded Greetings

*Angelic wings carry peace and love over the world* in this classical design by Lee Fisher. Stitched twice, this elegant piece will set the finest table of the holiday season.

**Project instructions begin on page 100.**

*Fill the room with candlelight from this illuminating design* by Green Ginger Designs. The careful use of metallic threads will catch the light and garner many compliments in your holiday home.

**Project instructions begin on page 102.**

# Gilded Greetings

*Experiment with a wide variety of Kreinik threads to create unique, glittering ornaments* for your Christmas tree. Dana Batho of Peacock and Fig has designed a set of delicate baubles you'll treasure.

**Project instructions begin on page 104.**

# Gilded Greetings

## Nativity Sampler

### Fabric

- Sampler: One 19" × 22" piece of 28-ct. Chocolate Raspberry Linen (stitched over two threads)
- Card: One 10" × 10" piece of 28-ct. Navy Brittney Lugana® (stitched over two threads)

### Design Size

- Sampler: 28-ct. = 10½" × 14"
- Card: 28-ct. = 3½" × 2⅞"

### Finishing Materials—Card

- Blank, 7" × 5" greeting card in coordinating color
- 7" × 5" piece of coordinating cardstock
- Pencil
- Craft knife
- Hot glue
- ⅛"-wide white and gold cording
- Double-sided tape

### Instructions—Sampler

Center the design and begin stitching over two fabric threads. Work cross-stitches, half stitches, and quarter stitches with two strands of cotton embroidery floss or Kreinik (fine) #8 braid. Work backstitches, straight stitches, and French knots with one strand of cotton embroidery floss or Kreinik (fine) #8 braid. Use a pressing cloth to carefully iron the needlework from the back before framing as desired.

### Instructions—Card

Center the 50w × 40h nativity design, omitting the ground and stable walls, and begin stitching over two threads. Work all stitches as for the sampler above. Use a pressing cloth to carefully iron the needlework from the back. Center and trim the finished needlework to 6" × 4½" and set aside.

Draw an approximately 5¼" × 3¾" oval in the center of the greeting card. Use a craft knife to carefully cut out the oval window. Wrap the cording around the oval twice, securing with hot glue every couple of inches.

Center the needlework in the oval window and affix to the back side of the cardstock with double-sided tape. Use double-sided tape to cover the back of the needlework with coordinating cardstock. Embellish as desired.

# Gilded
## Greetings

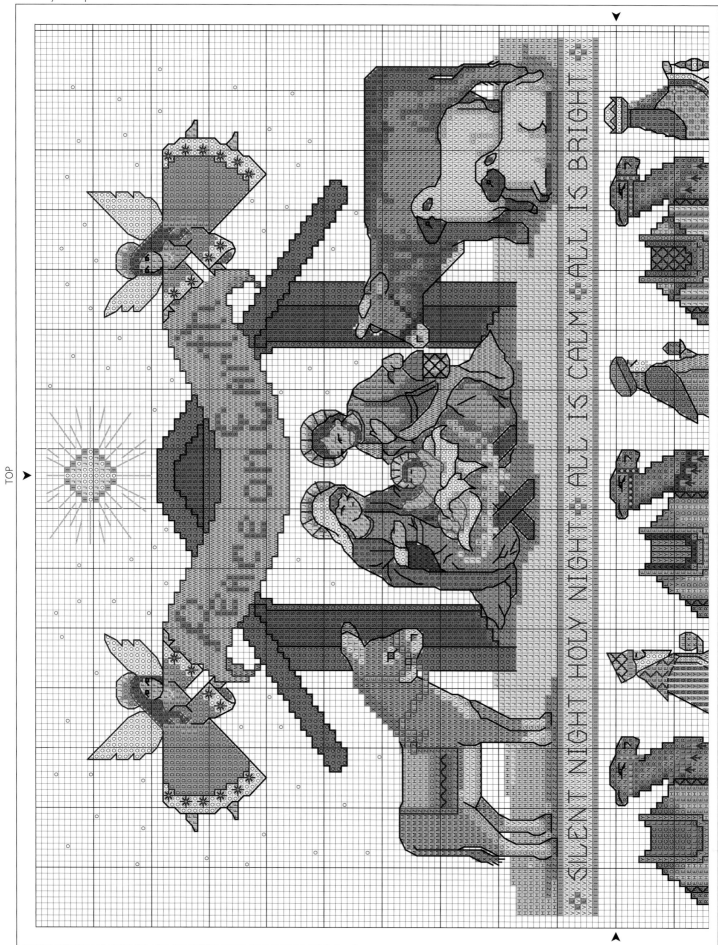

TOP

## CROSS-STITCH

| ANCHOR | | DMC | COLOR |
|---|---|---|---|
| 897 | A | 221 | Very Dark Shell Pink |
| 1049 | S | 301 | Medium Mahogany |
| 006 | T | 353 | Peach |
| 8581 | M | 646 | Dark Beaver Gray |
| 900 | G | 648 | Light Beaver Gray |
| 326 | C | 720 | Dark Orange Spice |
| 324 | E | 721 | Medium Orange Spice |
| 323 | D | 722 | Light Orange Spice |
| 302 | H | 743 | Medium Yellow |
| 301 | J | 744 | Pale Yellow |
| 275 | V | 746 | Off White |
| 907 | L | 832 | Golden Olive |
| 907 | K | 833 | Light Golden Olive |
| 4146 | F | 950 | Light Desert Sand |
| 1001 | Q | 976 | Medium Golden Brown |
| 1002 | N | 977 | Light Golden Brown |
| 1024 | Y | 3328 | Dark Salmon |
| 382 | X | 3371 | Black Brown |
| 896 | B | 3721 | Dark Shell Pink |
| 1048 | R | 3776 | Light Mahogany |
| 306 | Z | 3852 | Very Dark Straw |
| 311 | W | 3855 | Light Autumn Gold |
| 002 | O | 3865 | Winter White |

| KREINIK BRAID #8 | | COLOR |
|---|---|---|
| 002 | I | Gold |

## FRENCH KNOT

| ANCHOR | DMC | COLOR |
|---|---|---|
| 897 ● | 221 | Very Dark Shell Pink |
| 326 ● | 720 | Dark Orange Spice |
| 002 ● | 3865 | Winter White |

| KREINIK BRAID #8 | COLOR |
|---|---|
| 002 ● | Gold |

## BACKSTITCH

| ANCHOR | DMC | COLOR |
|---|---|---|
| 324 — | 721 | Medium Orange Spice |
| 382 — | 3371 | Black Brown |
| 311 — | 3855 | Light Autumn Gold |

## STRAIGHT STITCH

| ANCHOR | DMC | COLOR |
|---|---|---|
| 897 — | 221 | Very Dark Shell Pink |
| 1049 — | 301 | Medium Mahogany |
| 002 — | 3865 | Winter White |

| KREINIK BRAID #8 | COLOR |
|---|---|
| 002 — | Gold |

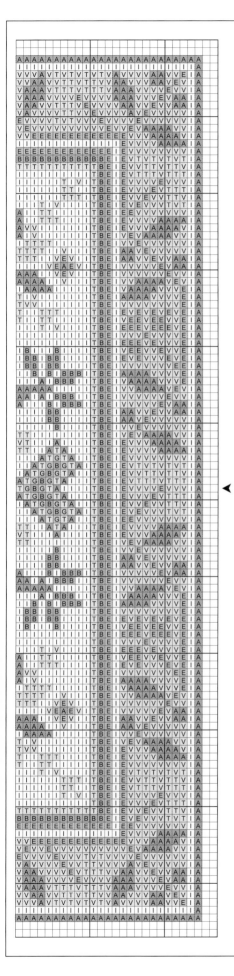

# Gilded Greetings

## Golden Snowflake Biscornu

### Fabric
- One 15" × 15" piece of 32-ct. White Belfast Linen (stitched over two threads)

### Design Size
- 32-ct. = 7" × 7"

### Finishing Materials
- 7½" × 7½" piece of white fabric
- Coordinating sewing thread
- Polyester fiberfill
- Two ½" buttons

### General Instructions
Center the design and begin stitching over two fabric threads. Work cross-stitches with two strands of cotton embroidery floss. Use a pressing cloth to carefully iron the needlework from the back before finishing.

### Finishing Instructions
Center and trim the needlework to 7½" × 7½". With wrong sides together and matching one corner of the needlework top to the halfway point on one side of the white fabric bottom, whipstitch the top and bottom together, leaving a 2" opening on one side. Turn, stuff with fiberfill and whipstitch the opening closed. Find the center of the bottom and sew through to the center of the top with two strands of coordinating floss. Add a button and return back through to the bottom. Attach a second button, pull taut, and pass through the buttons a few times. Tie off the thread on the bottom to secure and trim the excess.

### CROSS-STITCH

| ANCHOR | | DMC | COLOR |
|---|---|---|---|
| 1049 | G | 301 | Medium Mahogany |
| 045 | A | 814 | Dark Garnet |
| 390 | I | 822 | Light Beige Gray |
| 340 | T | 919 | Red Copper |
| 1015 | E | 3777 | Very Dark Terra Cotta |
| 901 | B | 3829 | Very Dark Old Gold |
| 306 | V | 3852 | Very Dark Straw |

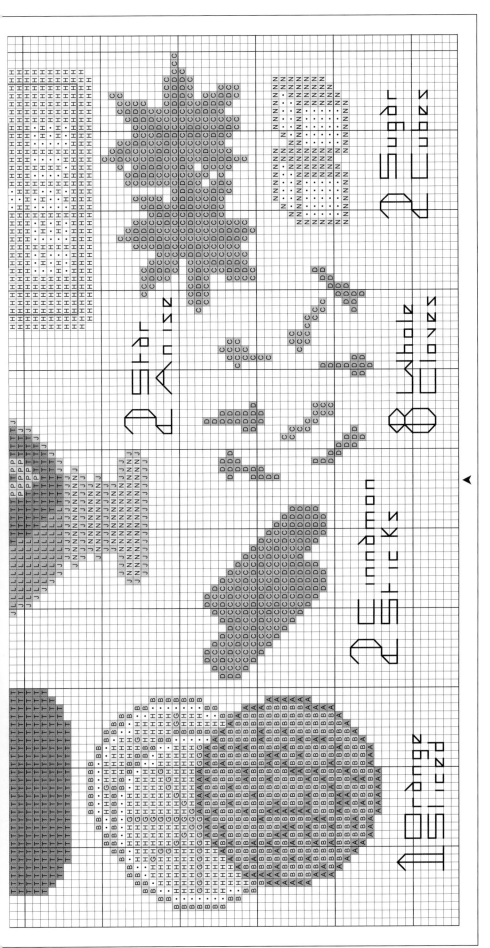

## Mulled Wine

### Fabric

- One 16" × 18" piece of 30-ct. Tiger's Eye Hand-Dyed Linen (stitched over two threads)

### Design Size

- 30-ct. = 7¼" × 9½"

### Instructions

Center the design and begin stitching over two fabric threads. Work cross-stitches with two strands of cotton embroidery floss. Work backstitches with one strand of cotton embroidery floss. Use a pressing cloth to carefully iron the needlework from the back before framing as desired.

### CROSS-STITCH

| ANCHOR | | DMC | COLOR |
|---|---|---|---|
| 002 | • | White | White |
| 969 | P | 152 | Medium Light Shell Pink |
| 362 | E | 437 | Light Tan |
| 1040 | J | 647 | Medium Beaver Gray |
| 227 | K | 701 | Light Christmas Green |
| 234 | N | 762 | Very Light Pearl Gray |
| 333 | A | 900 | Dark Burnt Orange |
| 1003 | B | 922 | Light Copper |
| 1027 | L | 3722 | Medium Shell Pink |
| 1048 | C | 3776 | Light Mahogany |
| 1015 | T | 3777 | Very Dark Terra Cotta |
| 306 | G | 3820 | Dark Straw |
| 305 | H | 3821 | Straw |
| 358 | D | 3862 | Dark Mocha Beige |

### BACKSTITCH

| ANCHOR | | DMC | COLOR |
|---|---|---|---|
| 002 | —— | White | White |
| 1015 | —— | 3777 | Very Dark Terra Cotta |

## Peach on Earth

### Fabric
- One 18" × 13" piece of 28-ct. Queen Anne's Lace Hand-Dyed Jobelan® (stitched over two threads)

### Design Size
- 28-ct. = 9¾" × 4¾"

### Finishing Materials
- 1¼ yards of ivory print fabric
- ¼ yard of gold fabric
- Two 9" × 15" pieces of lightweight fusible interfacing
- 14" × 45" piece of lightweight quilt batting
- Matching sewing thread

### General Instructions
Center the design and begin stitching over two fabric threads. Work cross-stitches and quarter stitches with two strands of cotton embroidery floss. Work backstitches and French knots with one strand of cotton embroidery floss. Use a pressing cloth to carefully iron the needlework from the back before finishing. To finish as a table runner as shown, stitch the design twice.

### Finishing Instructions
Use a ¼" seam allowance for all sewing unless specified. Center the interfacing on the wrong side of the needlework

and, following the manufacturer's instructions, fuse into place. Center and trim to 14" × 7¾".

Cut one 14" × 29½" piece of ivory print fabric. With wrong sides together, sew each short end of to the top edge of a piece of needlework. Press.

Cut a piece of ivory print fabric the same size as the table runner top. Place the top and bottom with right sides together and the edges aligned, with the batting on the wrong side of the bottom piece. Sew around all sides, leaving an opening for turning. Trim the corners diagonally and turn. Press well.

CROSS-STITCH

| ANCHOR | | DMC | COLOR |
|---|---|---|---|
| 977 | V | 334 | Medium Baby Blue |
| 891 | U | 676 | Light Old Gold |
| 886 | Z | 677 | Very Light Old Gold |
| 305 | D | 728 | Topaz |
| 890 | G | 729 | Medium Old Gold |
| 128 | A | 775 | Very Light Baby Blue |
| 307 | S | 783 | Medium Topaz |
| 132 | B | 797 | Royal Blue |
| 341 | H | 918 | Dark Red Copper |
| 1011 | Y | 948 | Very Light Peach |
| 1001 | E | 976 | Medium Golden Brown |

FRENCH KNOT

| ANCHOR | | DMC | COLOR |
|---|---|---|---|
| 341 | • | 918 | Dark Red Copper |

BACKSTITCH

| ANCHOR | | DMC | COLOR |
|---|---|---|---|
| 977 | —— | 334 | Medium Baby Blue |
| 305 | —— | 728 | Topaz |
| 132 | —— | 797 | Royal Blue |
| 341 | —— | 918 | Dark Red Copper |
| 1011 | —— | 948 | Very Light Peach |

## Project Tip

**Storing Seasonal Needlework**

Wrap seasonal items in acid-free tissue paper and place in an acid-free box for storage. (Plastic bags or bins can trap moisture.) Store the box in a dark place, free from humidity or extreme temperatures.

# Gilded
## Greetings

Cut 1½" strips of gold fabric and piece together to form a strip at least 121" long. Fold in half along the length with wrong sides together and press to create binding. With cut edges aligned and using a ¼" seam allowance, sew binding around the top side of the piece, folding to form a miter at each corner. Fold and press the binding to the back and hand-stitch in place.

Stitch Count = 121w × 123h

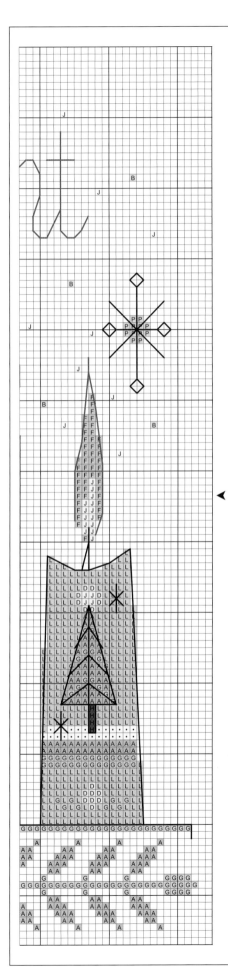

## Merry & Bright Candles

### Fabric
- One 17" × 17" piece of 14-ct. Black Chocolate Aida

### Design Size
- 14-ct. = 8⅝" × 8¾"

### Finishing Materials
- One 9" × 9" piece of self-adhesive mat board
- One 9½" × 9½" piece of self-adhesive mat board
- One 10" × 10" piece of self-adhesive mat board
- ½ yard of gold print fabric
- ½ yard of metallic red fabric
- Spray adhesive
- ¼"-wide gold ribbon
- Scissors

### General Instructions
Center the design and begin stitching. Work cross-stitches with two strands of cotton embroidery floss or DMC® Light Effects floss. Work backstitches and French knots with one strand of cotton embroidery floss. Use a pressing cloth to carefully iron the needlework from the back before finishing.

### Finishing Instructions
Trim the finished needlework to within 1½" on each side. Spray the wrong side of the needlework and the non-adhesive side of the 9" piece of mat board with spray adhesive. Center the matboard on the wrong side of the needlework and press in place. Remove the adhesive backing from the matboard, trim the corners of the needlework fabric, and fold the sides of the needlework to the back. Set aside.

Repeat this process with an 11" × 11" piece of gold print fabric and the 9½" piece of matboard and an 11½" × 11½" piece of metallic red fabric and the 10" piece of matboard.

Cut a 16" length of gold ribbon and affix the ends to the back of the red fabric-covered board, 2½" from the left and right edges. Cut a 10½" × 10½" piece of metallic red fabric.

Press the edges ¼" to the wrong side. Spray the wrong side with basting spray and place right-side up on the back of the red fabric-covered board, neatly covering the hanger.

Layer the three covered matboards in ascending size, using additional adhesive spray or other adhesive as desired.

# Gilded Greetings

### CROSS-STITCH

| ANCHOR | | DMC | COLOR |
|---|---|---|---|
| 002 | • | White | White |
| 1006 | G | 304 | Medium Christmas Red |
| 362 | K | 437 | Light Tan |
| 886 | L | 677 | Very Light Old Gold |
| 326 | A | 720 | Dark Orange Spice |
| 323 | B | 722 | Light Orange Spice |
| 301 | J | 744 | Pale Yellow |
| 045 | E | 814 | Dark Garnet |
| 1004 | N | 920 | Medium Copper |
| 332 | H | 946 | Medium Burnt Orange |
| 305 | D | 3821 | Straw |

| DMC LIGHT EFFECTS | | COLOR |
|---|---|---|
| E301 | P | Copper |
| E3821 | F | Light Gold |

### FRENCH KNOT

| ANCHOR | | DMC | COLOR |
|---|---|---|---|
| 002 | • | White | White |

### BACKSTITCH

| ANCHOR | | DMC | COLOR |
|---|---|---|---|
| 002 | —— | White | White |
| 400 | —— | 317 | Pewter Gray |

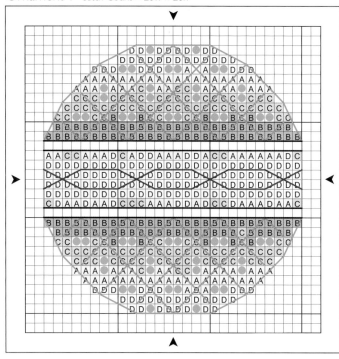

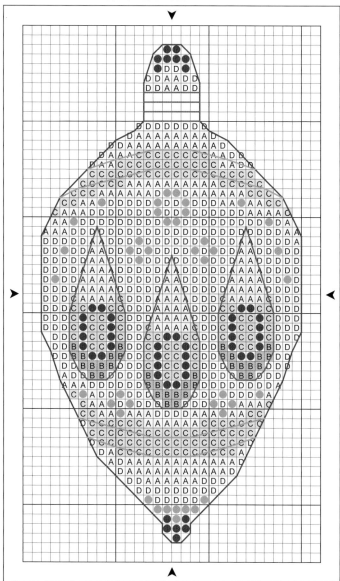

# Gilded Greetings

## Glittering Ornaments

### Fabric
### (each design)
- One 10" × 10" piece of 28-ct. Ivory Jobelan® (stitched over two threads)

### Design Size
- Ornament 1: 28-ct. = 2" × 2"
- Ornament 2: 28-ct. = 2" × 3¾"
- Ornament 3: 28-ct. = 2½" × 2½"
- Ornament 4: 28-ct. = 2" × 2"

### Embellishments
- One package each Old Gold #00557 and Ice #02010 glass seed beads from Mill Hill®
- One package Antique Ginger #03038 antique glass seed beads from Mill Hill

### Finishing Materials
- Four 3½" × 5½" pieces of self-adhesive foam mounting board
- Four 18" lengths of ⅛"-wide metallic gold trim
- Four 3½" × 5½" pieces of coordinating felt
- Clear quick-dry craft glue
- DMC® embroidery floss in color Ecru

### General Instructions
Center the design and begin stitching over two fabric threads. Work cross-stitches with two strands of cotton embroidery floss.

Work backstitches with 1 strand of Kreinik (tapestry) #12 braid or Kreinik ⅛" ribbon. Work couched backstitches with indicated number of strands of Kreinik (tapestry) #12 braid or Kreinik #7 Japan thread. Attach beads with 1 strand of coordinating floss. Lay the needlework facedown on a terry cloth towel (to protect beads) and use a pressing cloth to carefully iron the needlework from the back before finishing.

**Finishing Instructions**

Trim the mounting board into the shape of the finished needlework, ¾" wider than the finished design on all sides. Peel the protective paper from the mounting board. Center the foam side on the back of the needlework and press to stick. Trim excess fabric ½" beyond the edge of the board. Fold the edge of the fabric to the back and glue in place.

Position and glue the trim around the edge of the ornament so the ends meet at the top. Tie the ends of the trim together to form a hanger.

Wrap 1 undivided strand of Ecru embroidery floss around a book of your desired tassel length (model show is 5"). Continue wrapping until tassel is the desired fullness (model show was wrapped 15 times). Cut a 5" piece of floss and thread it beneath the wrapped floss at the top of the book. Tie a knot and remove the wrapped floss from the book. Cut the bottom of the looped strands. Wrap gold cording ½" down from the knot to create the "neck" of the tassel. Trim as desired.

Secure the knotted floss strand of the tassel to the back of the ornament so it hangs straight down. Use the finished needlework to cut a piece of felt the same shape. Glue felt to the back of the ornament.

### CROSS-STITCH

| ANCHOR | | DMC | COLOR |
|---|---|---|---|
| 926 | A | 712 | Cream |
| 361 | B | 738 | Very Light Tan |
| 387 | C | 739 | Ultra Very Light Tan |
| 002 | D | 3865 | Winter White |

### BACKSTITCH

| KREINIK RIB 1/8" | COLOR |
|---|---|
| 321J ▬ | Dark Gold |

| KREINIK BRAID #12 | COLOR |
|---|---|
| 321J ▬ | Dark Gold |

### STRAIGHT STITCH

| KREINIK BRAID #12 | COLOR |
|---|---|
| 321J ▬ | Dark Gold |

### BEAD

| MILL HILL GLASS SEED | | COLOR |
|---|---|---|
| 00557 | ● | Old Gold |
| 02010 | ● | Ice |
| 03038 | ● | Antique Ginger |

### COUCHING

| KREINIK JAPAN #7 | | COLOR |
|---|---|---|
| 002J | ▬ | Gold (1 strand) |
| 021J | ▬ | Copper (1 strand) |
| 002J | ▬ | Gold (2 strands) |
| 021J | ▬ | Copper (2 strands) |

| KREINIK BRAID #12 | | COLOR |
|---|---|---|
| 5804 | ▬ | Calypso (2 strands) |

*Note:* Not all colors are used in each design.

Ornament 3  Stitch Count = 34w × 34h

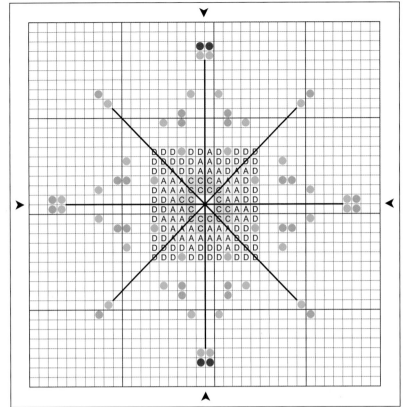

Project Tip

**Using Metallic Thread**

The use of a thread conditioner will reduce the wear on the thread as it passes through the fabric and the eye of the needle. It's also especially handy when threading the needle, as metallic threads often have a tendency to untwist at the cut ends.

Ornament 4  Stitch Count = 28w × 28h

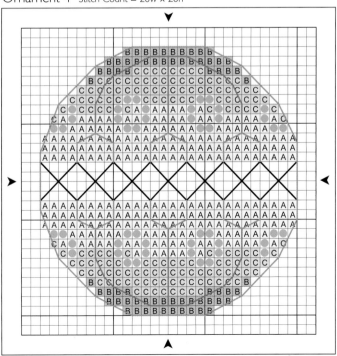

# No-Snow
# Christmas

*The only White Christmas you'll find in this chapter are the white, sandy beaches of the tropical coast.* Take off on a destination celebration with these playful designs that trade in hats and mittens for flip-flops and bathing suits. Send Santa's best with a set of "wish you were here" greeting cards designed by Lee Fisher or grab your stitching and relax in the sun with charming tropical bells, a fishbowl Frosty, or a palm-tree clothesline for Santa's suit. Take a break from snowflakes and frostbite with seashells and pool floaties!

**Project instructions begin on page 114.**

*Santa is officially on vacation in this breezy little design*
by Cheryl McKinnon. Encourage fun and relaxation this holiday season with
this reminder to take off the coat every once in a while.

**Project instructions begin on page 125.**

# No-Snow
# Christmas

*Build a snowman without
the snow in this clever design*
by Vinniey Tan. The little fish in this
holiday-themed home know how
to celebrate the season with the
best of them.

**Project instructions begin on page 116.**

*Capture a little holiday whimsy with these too-cute ornaments* designed by Laurel Blake. You are sure to get a huge, sunny smile when these characters come to stay.

**Project instructions begin on page 120.**

*Follow this driftwood sign* designed by Ursula Michael to your holiday hideaway on the beach. Share the gifts of sun, surf, and sand with your guests this Christmas season with this fun cross-stitch piece.

**Project instructions begin on page 118.**

# No-Snow
# Christmas

*Even this cheerful little crab is getting in the holiday spirit with his silly Santa outfit.* The bright colors and inventive script designed by Emma Congdon make this little box the best gift of the season.

**Project instructions begin on page 121.**

# No-Snow
# Christmas

*Capture some wildlife in their Christmas celebrations with these two brilliant snapshots* designed by Shannan Grierson. Careful use of half-stitches and shading give these bells beautiful detail.

**Project instructions begin on page 122.**

## Sea-Sun's Greetings   Stitch Count = 28w × 48h

## Happy Holidaze   Stitch Count = 34w × 49h

## Merry & Bright   Stitch Count = 34w × 47h

## Happy Holi-Rays   Stitch Count = 30w × 48h

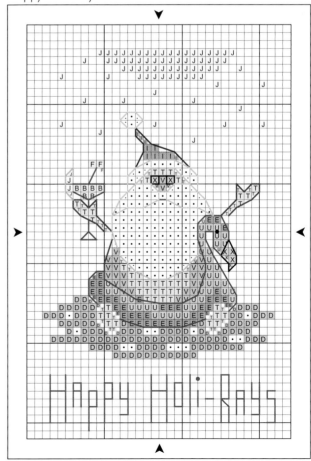

Sandy Clause  Stitch Count = 28w × 47h

# No-Snow **Christmas**

## Wish You Were Here Cards

### Fabric (each design)
• One 5½" × 6½" piece of 14-ct.
  Summer Sky Aida

### Design Size
• Sea-Sun's Greeting: 14-ct. = 2" × 3½"
• Happy Holidaze: 14-ct. = 2⅜" × 3½"
• Merry & Bright: 14-ct. = 2⅜" × 3⅜"
• Happy Holi-Rays: 14-ct. = 2⅛" × 3½"
• Sandy Clause: 14-ct. = 2" × 3⅜"

### Finishing Materials
• Greeting cards with 3¼" × 4¾" opening
• Coordinating cardstock
• Double-sided tape

### General Instructions
Center the design and begin stitching.
Work cross-stitches and quarter stitches
with two strands of cotton embroidery
floss. Work backstitches and French
knots with one strand of cotton
embroidery floss. Use a pressing
cloth to carefully iron the needlework
from the back before finishing.

### Finishing Instructions
Center and trim the needlework to within
1¼" from the edge of the stitching on each
side. Place double-sided tape around the
window opening on the wrong side of the
card front. Center the design in the window
and attach the right side of the needlework
fabric to the double-sided tape. Affix a
piece of cardstock on the inside of the
card, completely covering the needlework.

CROSS-STITCH

| ANCHOR | | DMC | COLOR |
|---|---|---|---|
| 002 | · | White | White |
| 403 | X | 310 | Black |
| 010 | A | 351 | Coral |
| 288 | J | 445 | Light Lemon |
| 098 | N | 553 | Violet |
| 830 | S | 644 | Medium Beige Gray |
| 238 | F | 703 | Chartreuse |
| 013 | I | 817 | Very Dark Coral Red |
| 380 | K | 838 | Very Dark Beige Brown |
| 257 | G | 905 | Dark Parrot Green |
| 186 | D | 959 | Medium Sea Green |
| 185 | B | 964 | Light Sea Green |

CROSS-STITCH

| ANCHOR | | DMC | COLOR |
|---|---|---|---|
| 006 | T | 967 | Very Light Apricot |
| 328 | V | 3341 | Apricot |
| 899 | C | 3782 | Light Mocha Brown |
| 062 | E | 3805 | Cyclamen Pink |
| 066 | U | 3806 | Light Cyclamen Pink |
| 358 | H | 3862 | Dark Mocha Beige |
| 379 | Y | 3863 | Medium Mocha Beige |

FRENCH KNOT

| ANCHOR | | DMC | COLOR |
|---|---|---|---|
| 403 | ● | 310 | Black |
| 358 | ● | 3862 | Dark Mocha Beige |

BACKSTITCH

| ANCHOR | | DMC | COLOR |
|---|---|---|---|
| 403 | —— | 310 | Black |
| 288 | —— | 445 | Light Lemon |
| 098 | —— | 553 | Violet |
| 238 | —— | 703 | Chartreuse |
| 013 | —— | 817 | Very Dark Coral Red |
| 186 | —— | 959 | Medium Sea Green |
| 006 | —— | 967 | Very Light Apricot |
| 899 | —— | 3782 | Light Mocha Brown |
| 062 | —— | 3805 | Cyclamen Pink |
| 358 | —— | 3862 | Dark Mocha Beige |

*Note:* Not all colors are used in each design.

## Fishbowl Frosty

**Fabric**
- One 15" × 19" piece of 14-ct. Sterling Hand-Dyed Aida

**Design Size**
- 14-ct. = 7⅛" × 11⅜"

**Finishing Materials**
- ½ yard of green print fabric

- 7½" × 12" piece of lightweight fusible interfacing
- 1 yard of green fringe trim
- Matching sewing thread
- 14" × 12" pillow form

**General Instructions**
Center the design and begin stitching. Work cross-stitches with two strands of

cotton embroidery floss. Use a pressing cloth to carefully iron the needlework from the back before finishing.

**Finishing Instructions**
Use a ¼" seam allowance for all sewing unless otherwise specified. Center and trim the needlework to 7½" × 12".

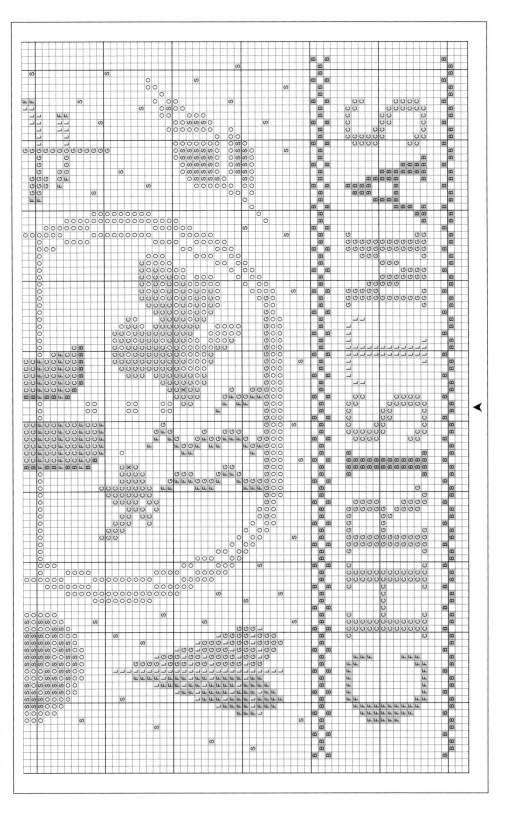

# No-Snow
# Christmas

## Project Tip

**Preventing Bleeding Onto Fabric**
Even colorfast floss may sometimes
bleed onto the fabric, and red floss
often does so. To prevent any
potential problems, pre-soak the
red thread in a mixture of 1 gallon
of water and 1 cup of white vinegar
to set the dyes. Allow the thread to
dry completely before stitching.

Center the interfacing on the wrong
side of the needlework and, following the
manufacturer's directions, fuse into place.

Cut two 4" × 12½" strips of green print
fabric. With right sides together, sew to
each side edge of the needlework. Press
toward the strips. Cut two 12" pieces of
green fringe trim.

Align over the seams just pressed
with the fringe away from the needlework
and sew in place.

Cut two 14½" × 18" pieces of green
print fabric for an envelope back. Fold
and press each in half with wrong sides
together to form two 14½" × 9" pieces.

Overlap the pieces to create a
pillow back that is the same size as
the front. Baste the overlapping pieces
in place. With right sides together,
sew the pillow back and front together.
Turn through the envelope opening
and insert a pillow form.

Sun, Surf, Sand Tree Stitch Count = 103w × 145h

TOP

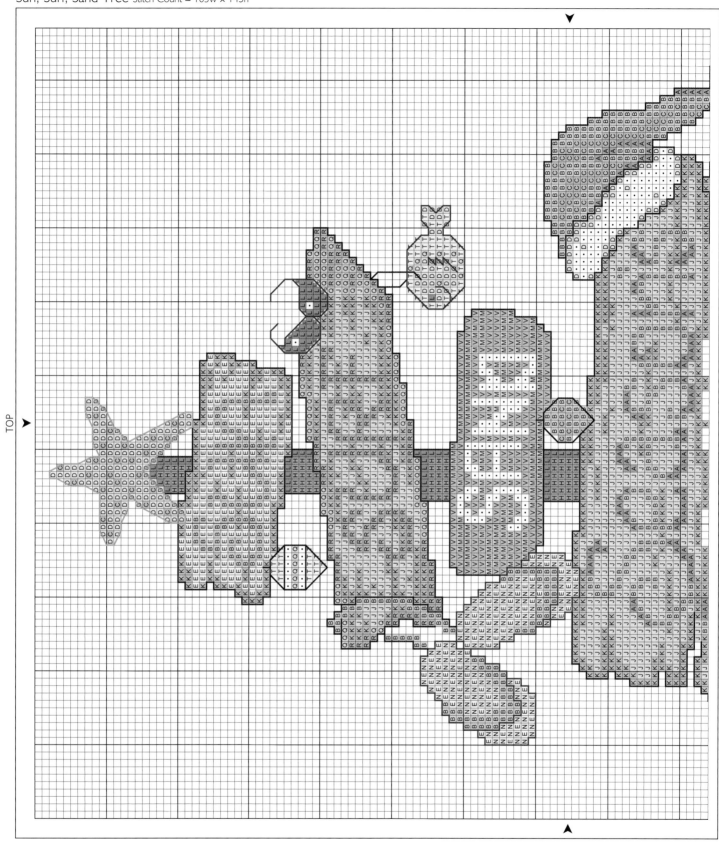

CROSS-STITCH

| ANCHOR | | DMC | COLOR |
|---|---|---|---|
| 002 | • | White | White |
| 9046 | B | 321 | Christmas Red |
| 010 | C | 351 | Coral |
| 006 | D | 353 | Peach |

CROSS-STITCH

| ANCHOR | | DMC | COLOR |
|---|---|---|---|
| 1046 | H | 435 | Very Light Brown |
| 362 | S | 437 | Light Tan |
| 830 | K | 644 | Medium Beige Gray |
| 228 | V | 700 | Bright Christmas Green |

CROSS-STITCH

| ANCHOR | | DMC | COLOR |
|---|---|---|---|
| 226 | M | 702 | Kelly Green |
| 293 | E | 727 | Very Light Topaz |
| 361 | F | 738 | Very Light Tan |
| 359 | L | 801 | Dark Coffee Brown |

CROSS-STITCH

| ANCHOR | | DMC | COLOR |
|---|---|---|---|
| 043 | A | 815 | Medium Garnet |
| 390 | J | 822 | Light Beige Gray |
| 255 | N | 907 | Light Parrot Green |

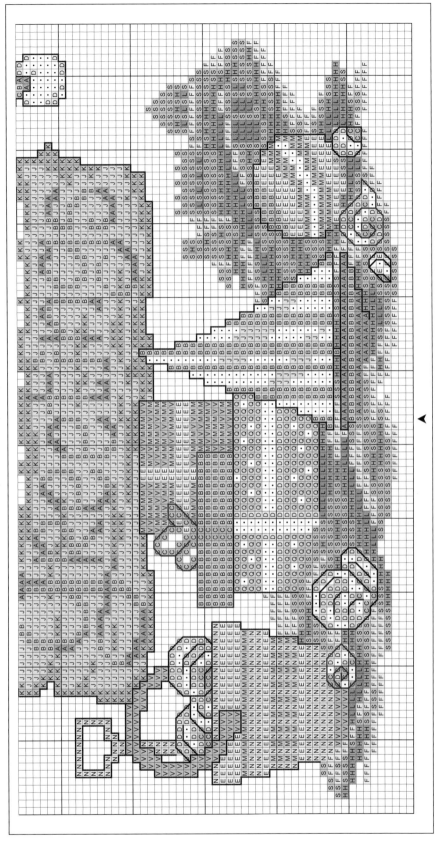

## Sun, Surf, Sand Tree

**Fabric**
- Framed: One 15" × 18" piece of 14-ct. Tropical Blue Aida
- Keychain: One 5" × 4" piece of 14-ct. Clear Perforated Plastic

**Design Size**
- Framed: 14-ct. = 7⅜" × 10⅜"
- Keychain: 14-ct. = 1½ " × 1⅓"

**Finishing Materials—Keychain**
- Stiff red felt
- Craft glue
- Jump ring
- Key ring
- Cork
- Flat thumbtack
- Coordinating floss

**Instructions—Framed**

Center the design and begin stitching.
Work cross-stitches and quarter stitches
with two strands of cotton embroidery floss.
Work backstitches and straight stitches
with one strand of cotton embroidery floss.
Use a pressing cloth to carefully iron the
needlework from the back before framing
as desired.

**Instructions—Keychain**

Section off the 20w × 19h starfish design,
center the design, and begin stitching.
Work cross-stitches with two strands of cotton
embroidery floss. Work backstitches with
one strand of cotton embroidery floss. Trim
the needlework to within 1 unstitched row.
Using the needlework as a guide, cut a felt
star from red felt ⅛" larger than the stitching.
Insert a jump ring through a top stitch of
the needlework and close around a key ring.
Insert a thumbtack in the top of a cork.
Knot floss around the thumbtack and
through the keyring to connect.

| CROSS-STITCH | | | BACKSTITCH | | | STRAIGHT STITCH | | |
|---|---|---|---|---|---|---|---|---|
| ANCHOR | DMC | COLOR | ANCHOR | DMC | COLOR | ANCHOR | DMC | COLOR |
| 187 | Q 958 | Dark Sea Green | 830 —— 644 | | Medium Beige Gray | 359 —— 801 | | Dark Coffee Brown |
| 185 | T 964 | Light Sea Green | 359 —— 801 | | Dark Coffee Brown | | | |
| 188 | R 3812 | Very Dark Sea Green | | | | | | |

**Flip Flops** Stitch Count = 30w × 32h

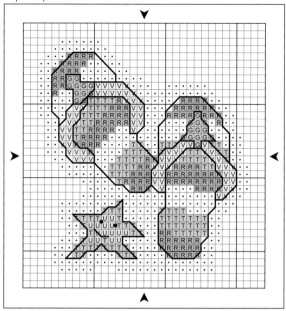

**Pool Toy** Stitch Count = 41w × 36h

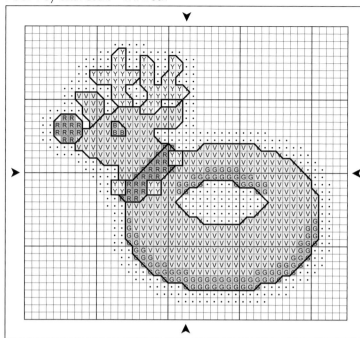

**Flamingo** Stitch Count = 24w × 41h

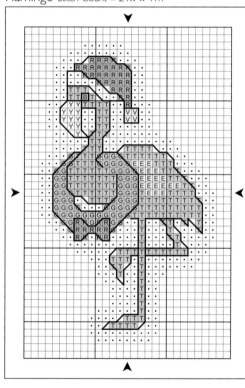

## Poolside Ornaments

### Fabric (each design)
- One 6" × 6" piece of 14-ct. White Perforated Plastic

### Design Size
- Flip Flops: 14-ct. = 2⅛" × 2¼"
- Flamingo: 14-ct. = 1¾" × 3"
- Pool Toy: 14-ct. = 3" × 2½"

### Finishing Materials (each design)
- 4" × 4" piece of coordinating felt
- Clear quick-dry craft glue
- 5" piece of coordinating ribbon

### Instructions
Center the design and begin stitching. Work cross-stitches with two strands of cotton embroidery floss. Work backstitches and French knots with one strand of cotton embroidery floss. Trim the finished needlework to within one unstitched row on all sides. Affix ribbon to the top back of each design for a hanger. Center and affix the felt to the back of the needlework. Trim the felt to within ⅛" of the needlework.

## Project Tip

**Create Fun Package Tags**

These cute patterns would also make great tags to decorate holiday presents—family and friends will delight over the playful designs!

# No-Snow Christmas

| CROSS-STITCH | | | |
|---|---|---|---|
| ANCHOR | | DMC | COLOR |
| 002 | · | White | White |
| 006 | U | 353 | Peach |
| 046 | R | 666 | Bright Christmas Red |
| 228 | G | 700 | Bright Christmas Green |
| 238 | V | 703 | Chartreuse |
| 305 | Y | 725 | Medium Light Topaz |
| 1021 | E | 761 | Light Salmon |
| 381 | B | 938 | Ultra Dark Coffee Brown |

| CROSS-STITCH | | | |
|---|---|---|---|
| ANCHOR | | DMC | COLOR |
| 033 | T | 3706 | Medium Melon |

| FRENCH KNOT | | | |
|---|---|---|---|
| ANCHOR | | DMC | COLOR |
| 381 | ● | 938 | Ultra Dark Coffee Brown |

| BACKSTITCH | | | |
|---|---|---|---|
| ANCHOR | | DMC | COLOR |
| 381 | — | 938 | Ultra Dark Coffee Brown |

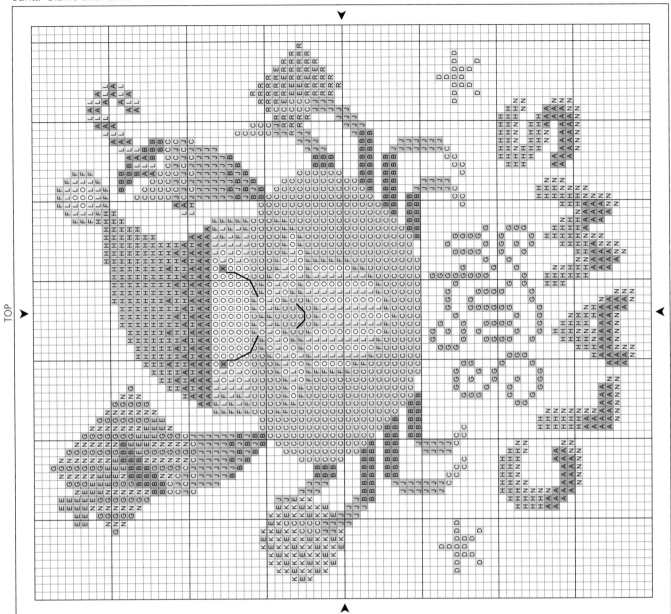

## Santa Claws

### Fabric
- One 13" × 14" piece of 28-ct. Sand Hand-Dyed Cashel (stitched over two threads)

### Design Size
- 28-ct. = 4⅞" × 5⅜"

### Finishing Materials
- Wooden box with 8" × 8" lid
- 6¼" × 6½" piece of mat board
- 26" length of ¾"-wide rope
- Rope scraps for embellishments
- Basting spray
- Clear quick-dry craft glue

### General Instructions
Center the design and begin stitching over two fabric threads. Work cross-stitches with two strands of cotton embroidery floss. Work backstitches with one strand of cotton embroidery floss. Use a pressing cloth to carefully iron the needlework from the back before finishing.

### Finishing Instructions
Trim the needlework to within 2" of the stitching on all sides. Lightly spray the mat board with basting spray and place glue-side down on the wrong side of the needlework. Glue the edges of the fabric to the back. Allow to dry. Affix the wrapped needlework to the top of the wooden box. Glue rope around the edge of the mat board, trimming the excess. Embellish with knots or bows of excess rope as desired.

### CROSS-STITCH

| ANCHOR | | DMC | COLOR |
|---|---|---|---|
| 231 | F | 005 | Light Driftwood |
| 403 | X | 310 | Black |
| 011 | A | 350 | Medium Coral |
| 010 | H | 351 | Coral |
| 238 | K | 703 | Chartreuse |
| 304 | D | 741 | Medium Tangerine |
| 923 | E | 909 | Very Dark Emerald Green |
| 340 | B | 919 | Red Copper |
| 1003 | J | 921 | Copper |
| 1003 | C | 922 | Light Copper |
| 187 | G | 958 | Dark Sea Green |
| 185 | N | 964 | Light Sea Green |
| 086 | R | 3608 | Very Light Plum |
| 002 | O | 3865 | Winter White |
| 926 | L | 3866 | Ultra Very Light Mocha Brown |

### BACKSTITCH

| ANCHOR | DMC | COLOR |
|---|---|---|
| 403 | —— 310 | Black |

## Tropical Bells

### Fabric (each design)
- One 14" × 15" piece of 30-ct. Morris Blue Linen (stitched over two threads)

### Design Size
- 30-ct. = 5⅝" × 6⅞"

### Finishing Materials
- ½ yard of red print fabric
- 1½ yards of ¼"-wide cording
- Polyester stuffing
- Matching sewing thread

### General Instructions
Center the design and begin stitching over two fabric threads. Work cross-stitches and quarter stitches with two strands of cotton embroidery floss. Work backstitches and French knots with one strand of cotton embroidery floss. Use a pressing cloth to carefully iron the needlework from the back before finishing.

### Finishing Instructions
Use a ¼" seam allowance for all sewing unless otherwise specified. Center and trim the needlework to within 1½" of the stitching, maintaining the bell shape. With wrong sides together, use this as a template to cut a red print fabric back. Set the back aside.

Cut 1½"-wide bias strips of the needlework fabric and piece together to form one 26"-long strip. Fold in half lengthwise with wrong sides together. Insert cording into the fold and sew tightly along the edge of the cording using a zipper foot. Maintaining the bell shape, start at the bottom of the needlework and sew the piping around the needlework, keeping the seam close to the cording.

Cut a 2¾" × 26½" piece of red print fabric. With rights side together, sew the short ends together to form a loop. Pin the fabric loop to the needlework with right sides together and sew around, sewing tight to the cording around the entire piece. Sew the back piece to the loop in the same manner, leaving an opening along the bottom for turning. Turn the piece right side out, stuff with fiberfill, and whipstitch the opening closed.

### CROSS-STITCH

| ANCHOR | | DMC | COLOR |
|---|---|---|---|
| 002 | · | White | White |
| 401 | B | 413 | Dark Pewter Gray |
| 398 | P | 415 | Pearl Gray |
| 943 | T | 422 | Light Hazelnut Brown |
| 1005 | S | 498 | Dark Christmas Red |
| 046 | J | 666 | Bright Christmas Red |
| 886 | A | 677 | Very Light Old Gold |
| 295 | Q | 726 | Light Topaz |
| 304 | Z | 741 | Medium Tangerine |
| 234 | H | 762 | Very Light Pearl Gray |
| 944 | N | 869 | Very Dark Hazelnut Brown |
| 255 | E | 907 | Light Parrot Green |
| 923 | C | 909 | Very Dark Emerald Green |
| 205 | L | 911 | Medium Emerald Green |
| 204 | R | 913 | Medium Nile Green |
| 4146 | U | 950 | Light Desert Sand |

### CROSS-STITCH

| ANCHOR | | DMC | COLOR |
|---|---|---|---|
| 185 | I | 964 | Light Sea Green |
| 298 | M | 972 | Dark Canary |
| 035 | G | 3801 | Light Christmas Red |
| 373 | W | 3828 | Hazelnut Brown |
| 410 | F | 3844 | Dark Bright Turquoise |
| 1090 | V | 3846 | Light Bright Turquoise |

### FRENCH KNOT

| ANCHOR | | DMC | COLOR |
|---|---|---|---|
| 002 | ● | White | White |
| 295 | ● | 726 | Light Topaz |

### BACKSTITCH

| ANCHOR | | DMC | COLOR |
|---|---|---|---|
| 401 | —— | 413 | Dark Pewter Gray |
| 295 | —— | 726 | Light Topaz |

*Note:* Not all colors are used in each design.

## Project Tip

### Preventing Twisting
During the movement of stitching, the needle naturally twists which can cause loops and knots in the thread. To prevent this, work several stitches, then make note of which way the thread unwinds when you hang it straight down from your work. Give your needle a partial turn in that direction with each stitch to keep the thread from twisting.

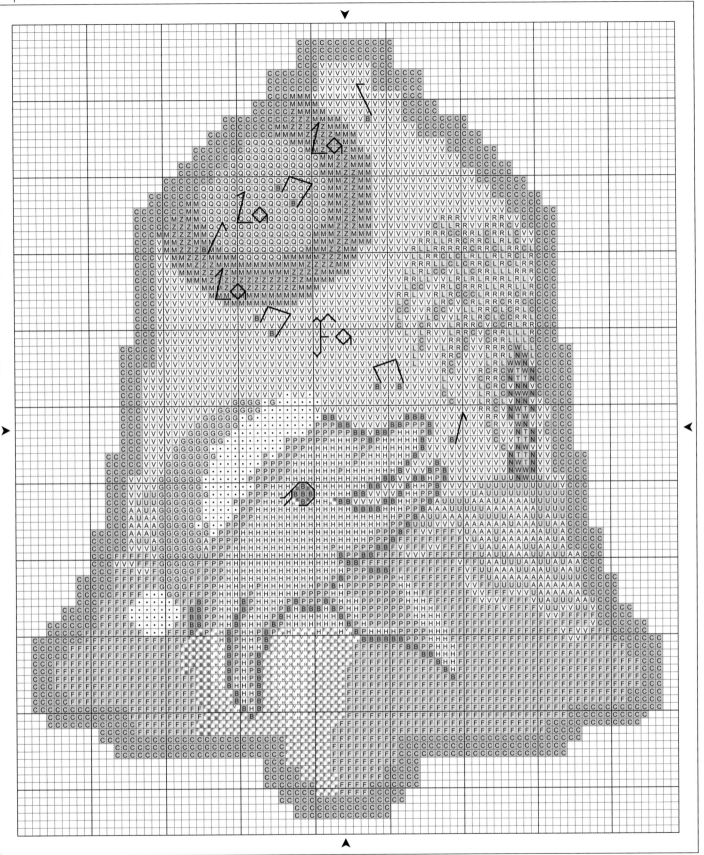

# No-Snow **Christmas**

# No-Snow Christmas

## Santa's Clothesline

### Fabric
• One 15" × 14" piece of 14-ct. Bluebell Aida

### Design Size
• 14-ct. = 7⅜" × 5⅝"

### General Instructions
Center the design and begin stitching.
Work cross-stitches with two strands of
cotton embroidery floss. Work backstitches
with one strand of cotton embroidery floss.
Use a pressing cloth to carefully iron the
needlework from the back before finishing.

### Finishing Instructions
Trim the needlework to within six unstitched rows.
Pull out two rows of fabric threads on all sides to
fringe the edges, leaving four unstitched rows on
all sides. Clip in pre-finished frame as desired.

CROSS-STITCH

| ANCHOR | | DMC | COLOR |
|--------|---|------|-------|
| 001 | O | B5200 | Snow White |
| 9046 | V | 321 | Christmas Red |
| 295 | Y | 726 | Light Topaz |
| 277 | M | 831 | Medium Golden Olive |
| 907 | I | 832 | Golden Olive |
| 874 | H | 834 | Very Light Golden Olive |
| 257 | C | 905 | Dark Parrot Green |
| 256 | J | 906 | Medium Parrot Green |
| 255 | A | 907 | Light Parrot Green |
| 186 | E | 959 | Medium Sea Green |
| 035 | R | 3801 | Light Christmas Red |

BACKSTITCH

| ANCHOR | DMC | COLOR |
|--------|-----|-------|
| 236 | 3799 | Very Dark Pewter Gray |

# Cross-Stitch Basics

## Getting Started

The written instructions for each project indicate where to begin stitching. For most projects, the starting point is at the center. Every chart has arrows that indicate the horizontal and vertical centers. With your finger, trace along the grid to the point where the two centers meet. Compare a symbol at the center of the chart to the key and choose which floss color to stitch first. To find the center of the fabric, fold it into quarters and finger-crease or baste along he folds with a single strand of contrasting floss. Cut the floss into 15" lengths and separate all six strands. Recombine the strands indicated in the project instructions and thread them into a blunt-tip needle.

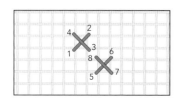

### Basic Cross-Stitch

Make one cross-stitch for each symbol on the chart. For horizontal rows, stitch the first diagonal of each stitch in the row. Work back across the row, completing each stitch. On most linen and evenweave fabrics, work the stitches over two threads as shown in the diagram above. For aida cloth, each stitch fills one square.

You also can work cross-stitches in the reverse direction. Remember to embroider the stitches uniformly— that is, always work the top half of each stitch in the same direction.

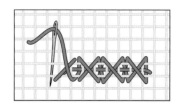

### To Secure Thread at the Beginning

The most common way to secure the beginning tail of the thread is to hold it under the first four or five stitches.

To secure the thread with a waste knot, thread the needle and knot the end of the thread. Insert the needle from the right side of the fabric, about 4" away from the first stitch. Bring the needle up through the fabric and work the first series of stitches. When finished, clip the knot on the right side. Rethread the needle with the excess floss and push the needle through to the stitches on the wrong side of the fabric.

When working with two, four, or six strands of floss, use a loop knot. Cut half as many strands of thread, making each one twice as long. Recombine the strands, fold the strands in half, and thread all of the ends into the needle. Work the first diagonal of the first stitch and slip the needle through the loop formed by folding the thread.

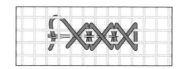

### To Secure Thread at the End

To finish, slip the threaded needle under the previously stitched threads on the wrong side of the fabric for four or five stitches, weaving the thread back and forth a few times. Clip the thread.

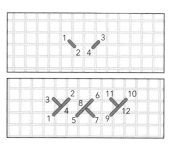

### Quarter and Three-Quarter Cross-Stitch

To obtain rounded shapes in a design, use quarter and three-quarter cross-stitches. On linen and evenweave fabrics, a quarter cross-stitch will extend from one corner to the center intersection of the threads. To make quarter cross-stitches on aida cloth, estimate the center of the square. Three-quarter cross-stitches combine a quarter cross-stitch with a half cross-stitch. Both stitches may slant in any direction.

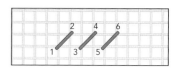

### Half Cross-Stitch

A half cross-stitch is a single diagonal or half a cross-stitch. They are indicated on the chart by a diagonal colored symbol unless otherwise indicated.

### Algerian Eyelet

The key to making this spoked stitch with its center hole is to work from the outside in. Bring the needle from the

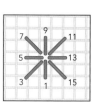

back to the front at an outside edge of the stitch, then push it to the back at the midpoint of the stitch, pulling the thread firmly and gently. As you work successive spokes, an opening will appear in the middle.

## Backstitch

Backstitches define and outline the shapes of a design. For most projects, backstitches require only one strand of floss.

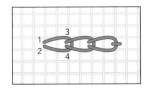

## Chain Stitch

Bring the needle to the front of the fabric and return to the back through the same hole, forming a loop. Slide the tip of the needle under two or more threads and bring it to the front of the fabric. Slip the loop under the needle tip. Pull gently until the loop lies smoothly on the fabric. Pass the needle to the back, forming the loop of the second stitch of the chain.

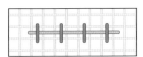

## Couching

Use two needles to work a line of couching. Bring the heavier couched thread through the fabric at the beginning of the line designated on the chart and to the back at the end. Roughly align it in the position indicated on the chart. Bring the thinner couching thread through the fabric four threads (unless otherwise specified on the chart) beyond the entry point of the couched thread, over it, and to the back in the next hole. Move four threads along the line of the couched thread and repeat the couching. Continue along the entire length of the couched thread.

## Cross-Stitch With Beads

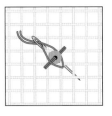

Beads may be attached by working the first half of each cross-stitch and attaching a bead on the return stitch.

Another method, to ensure that beads stand up straight, is to work with two strands of floss and add the bead to the first half-stitch. As you work the second diagonal, split the strands so one strand lies on each side of the bead.

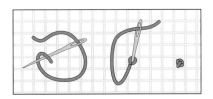

## French Knot

Bring the threaded needle through the fabric and wrap the floss around the needle as shown. Tighten the twists and return the needle through the fabric in the same place. The floss will slide through the wrapped thread to make the knot.

## Lazy Daisy

Bring the needle to the front of the fabric and return to the back through the same hole, forming a loop. Slide the tip of the needle under two or more threads, then bring it to the front of the fabric. Slip the loop under the needle tip. Pull gently until the loop lies smoothly on the fabric. Push the needle to the back, forming a tack stitch over the end of the loop.

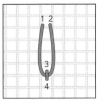

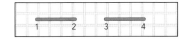

## Running Stitch

Running stitches work up fast and add design definition. They are usually equal in length, although uneven stitches create a novelty effect.

## Satin Stitch

This smooth-surface stitch may be worked over a few or many threads. Bring the needle up through the first hole. Count threads along a straight line and return to the back of the fabric. For the second stitch, bring the needle up through the hole immediately next to the first stitch.

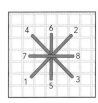

## Smyrna Cross

A Smyrna cross consists of an X-shape stitch topped by a straight vertical stitch and a straight horizontal stitch. It's often worked over four, six, eight, or more threads.

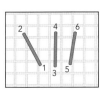

## Straight Stitch

The simplest of all stitches, straight stitches are often used for sun rays, whiskers, and other simple accents.

# Sources

*Many of the materials and items used in this book are available at needlework and craft stores. For more information, contact the manufacturers or suppliers listed below.*

## FABRICS

Lakeside Linens & Designs, Inc., PO Box 165, Clear Lake, WA 98235-0165; 360-428-8688; *www.lakesidelinens.com*

Picture This Plus, 212 N. Broadway Street, Abilene, KS 67410; 866-314-4343; *www.picturethisplus.com*

Ship's Manor, *www.shipsmanor.com*, shipsmanor@gmail.com

Weeks Dye Works, Inc., 1510-103 Mechanical Boulevard, Garner, NC 27529; 877-OVERDYE; *www.weeksdyeworks.com*

Wichelt Imports, Inc., N162 Highway 35, Stoddard, WI 54658; *www.wichelt.com*, wichelt@wichelt.com

Zweigart®, Distributed by Herrschners®, 2800 Hoover Road, Stevens Point, WI 54481; 800-441-0838; *www.herrschners.com*

## FIBERS/THREADS

Anchor, Spinrite® LP, 320 Livingstone Avenue South, Listowel, OH Canada N4W 3H3; 888-308-8401; *www.yarninspirations.com*

The DMC Corporation, 86 Northfield Avenue, Edison, NJ 08837; 800-275-4117; *www.dmc.com/us/*

The Gentle Art, PO Box 670, New Albany, OH 43054; 614-855-8346; *www.thegentleart.com*

Kreinik Mfg., PO Box 1966, Parkersburg, WV 26102; 800-537-2166; *www.kreinik.com*

Weeks Dye Works, 1510-103 Mechanical Boulevard, Garner, NC 27529; 877-OVERDYE; *www.weeksdyeworks.com*

## PERFORATED PAPER & PLASTIC

Darice®, 13000 Darice Parkway, Strongsville, OH 44149; 866-432-7423; *www.darice.com*

Wichelt Imports, Inc., N162 Highway 35, Stoddard, WI 54658; *www.wichelt.com*

## EMBELLISHMENTS & FINISHING PRODUCTS

Herrschners, Inc, 2800 Hoover Road, Stevens Point, WI 54481; 800-441-0838; *www.herrschners.com*

Mill Hill, Wichelt Imports, Inc., N162 Highway 35, Stoddard, WI 54658; *www.wichelt.com*

## FRAMING

Koerten's Fine Framing and Gifts, 2501 Church Street, Stevens Point, WI 54481; 800-873-0056; *www.koertens.com*

## CHAPTER 1—CELEBRATING SANTA

*Merry Christmas Santa,* pages 6-7: Natural Brown Linen—Wichelt Imports.

*Jolly Santa Bookmarks,* page 8: Natural Brown Aida—Zweigart.

*Forest Santa Stocking,* page 9: White Aida—Zweigart.

*Classic Santa Portrait,* page 10: Ivory Jobelan—Wichelt Imports.

*Primitive Santa Tins,* page 11: Lambswool Jobelan—Wichelt Imports.

*Skating Claus Snow Globe,* page 12: Twilight Cashel—Picture This Plus. Beads—Mill Hill.

## CHAPTER 2—PLAYFUL PALETTE

*A Very Merry Christmas,* pages 24-25: White Cashel—Zweigart.

*Holiday Turtlenecks,* page 26: Antique Brown Perforated Paper—Wichelt Imports. Beads—Mill Hill.

*Polar Bear Under Glass,* page 27: Tropical Green Aida—Wichelt Imports.

*Season's Greetings Sleigh,* page 28: Wood Violet Jobelan—Wichelt Imports.

*Holly Bird Globe,* page 29: Vintage Winter Sky Linen—Lakeside Linens. Beads—Mill Hill.

*Fa La La La La,* page 30: Navy Aida—Zweigart.

*Home for X-Mas,* page 31: White Aida—Zweigart.

## CHAPTER 3—OLIVE & MERLOT

*Tiny Treasures,* pages 44-45: Clear Perforated Plastic—Darice.

*Noel Hoop,* page 46: Antique White Cashel—Zweigart. Beads—Mill Hill.

*Victorian Christmas,* page 47: Doubloon Hand-Dyed Cashel—Picture This Plus. Beads—Mill Hill.

*3-D Trees,* page 48: Clear Perforated Plastic—Darice.

*Caroling Kitties,* page 49: White Belfast Linen—Zweigart.

*Crimson Birds,* page 50: Soft Cream Belfast Linen—Zweigart.

## CHAPTER 4—PRETTY PASTELS

*Queen of the North,* pages 64-65: Sprite Cashel—Picture This Plus. Beads—Mill Hill.

*The Nutcracker Trio,* page 66: White Aida—Zweigart. Beads—Mill Hill.

*Merry Christmas Angel,* page 67: Angel Blush Lugana—Wichelt Imports. Hanger—Herrschners.

*Scrolling Merry Christmas,* page 68: White Aida—Zweigart.

*Woodland Animal Minis,* page 69: Bo Peep Pink Aida—Zweigart.

*I Saw Three Ships,* page 70: Beachy Keen Aida—Ship's Manor.

*Poinsettias & Snowflakes,* page 71: White Lugana—Zweigart.

## CHAPTER 5—GILDED GREETINGS

*Nativity Sampler,* pages 86-87: Chocolate Raspberry Linen—Wichelt Imports.

*Golden Snowflake Biscornu,* page 88: White Belfast Linen—Zweigart.

*Mulled Wine,* page 89: Tiger's Eye Linen—Weeks Dye Works.

*Merry & Bright Candles,* page 90: Black Chocolate Aida—Wichelt Imports.

*Peace on Earth,* page 91: Queen Anne's Lace Hand-Dyed Jobelan—Wichelt Imports.

*Glittering Ornaments,* page 92: Ivory Jobelan—Wichelt Imports. Beads—Mill Hill.

## CHAPTER 6—NO-SNOW CHRISTMAS

*Wish You Were Here Cards,* pages 106-107: Summer Sky Aida—Wichelt Imports.

*Santa's Clothesline,* page 108: Bluebell Aida—Wichelt Imports.

*Fishbowl Frosty,* page 109: Sterling Hand-Dyed Aida—Picture This Plus.

*Sun, Surf, Sand Tree,* page 110: Tropical Blue Aida—Wichelt Imports.

*Poolside Ornaments,* page 111: White Perforated Plastic—Darice.

*Santa Claws,* page 112: Sand Hand-Dyed Cashel—Picture This Plus.

*Tropical Bells,* page 113: Morris Blue Linen—Weeks Dye Works.